BULLET FOR MY VALENTINE

SCREAM AIM CONQUER

BEN WELCH

MUSIC
PRESS

Published by Music Press Books
an imprint of John Blake Publishing Ltd
3 Bramber Court, 2 Bramber Road,
London W14 9PB, England

www.johnblakebooks.com

www.facebook.com/johnblakebooks 🇫
twitter.com/jblakebooks 🇪

First published in Paperback in 2016

ISBN: 978-1-78418-981-5

British Library Cataloguing-in-Publication Data:

A catalogue record for this book is available from the British Library.

Design by www.envydesign.co.uk

Printed in Great Britain by CPI Group (UK) Ltd

3 5 7 9 10 8 6 4 2

Papers used by John Blake Publishing are natural, recyclable products made from
wood grown in sustainable forests. The manufacturing processes conform to the
environmental regulations of the country of origin.

Every attempt has been made to contact the relevant copyright-holders, but some were
unobtainable. We would be grateful if the appropriate people could contact us.

CONTENTS

INTRODUCTION

In garages, basements, school halls, churches and youth clubs up and down this and plenty of other countries, teenagers have gathered to play music together. Most of them won't get beyond playing for a few friends, with practise amps drowned out beneath an out-of-tune drum kit. Some will go further, playing pubs and small clubs for a local following before fizzling out with a couple of demos to prove that they existed. But all will fantasise about the big-time; that possibly extinct or maybe always fictional place where their idols will come to consider them peers and a new legion of fans will come to idolise them in turn. A place where glory and money come easily, the guitar is never out of style and 10,000 tickets for an arena show will sell out in twenty minutes. But in the early 1990s the big-time and Bridgend in Wales were not well acquainted.

Yet, somehow, in 2006 a young man from Bridgend was sitting on stage at the Tallinn Song Festival Grounds in Estonia. The grounds were the site of a traditional festival of national significance to the Estonians but they were also used as land-for-hire for large-scale concerts and tonight Metallica were playing. It was perfectly clear that day at the site, nestled in the Bay of Tallinn, with Helsinki just ninety kilometres across the Gulf of Finland – so from behind his kit, with the sun not yet set, Michael 'Moose' Thomas had an uninterrupted view of the 105,000 people that had come for Metallica. And the gig had a special significance for him and his band too. Metallica were the band that they had idolised as teenagers. Just a few years ago they were memorising their riffs in bedrooms, covering their songs in cramped rehearsal spaces, learning the cut and thrust of a heavy metal song as practised by the masters of the form. They had been on a band outing in 1996 to see Metallica play on the *Load* tour. And now not only were they supporting them at their own show but, as Moose looked to the side of the stage, he could see Lars Ulrich and James Hetfield watching their set. He forced himself to keep his eyes forward. It was all he could to keep his concentration. And yet, as the middle eight of his band's biggest single to date crashed in, he couldn't help but sneak a glance. Lars and James were playing air guitar. It was better than even a boyhood fantasy would dare to allow.

That night, Bullet for My Valentine would even make an onstage appearance during Metallica's set – a stamp of approval from one of the biggest heavy metal bands that the world has ever known. But Bullet had only just begun. Their own take on the classic thrash template of the early 1980s had already brought them in front of one of the world's largest gatherings of metalheads and it would take them even further, ultimately seeing them carve out their own place in the pantheon of the fast and the ferocious. But first, there was Bridgend.

CHAPTER ONE

TO BE BORN IN WALES

Bridgend sits in the south of Wales, around twenty miles west of the capital Cardiff. Bisected by the River Ogmore, its history, like much of South Wales, has been shaped by the fickle fortunes of industry – in particular, coal and steel. The soil of the valleys to the north of the town were so rich with coal that, by the time the First World War broke out, the small communities that speckled the mountainous terrain had swollen inexorably, with row upon row of terraced houses built to accommodate the influx of workers. But while at one time Cardiff and Swansea were some of the most important trade routes in the world for coal and steel, after the Second World War the industry entered a steady decline. First came dwindling investment from the government, before the free-market policies of Margaret

Thatcher in the 1980s effectively saw support being with-drawn altogether. The legacy of this sudden collapse was unemployment, deprivation and drug use.

Bridgend was not the worst hit of the South Wales towns, particularly thanks to the construction of a new motorway in the 1970s that connected the town with the east and the development of new, privately-owned housing estates in the 1980s. But as the 1980s turned into the 1990s, it was still marked by the residual problems of the valleys – a lack of jobs and a shortage of investment. However, all was not as hopeless as it seemed. As a verse from Brian Harris's famous poem *In Passing* goes, 'To be born in Wales, / Not with a silver spoon in your mouth, / But, with music in your blood / And with poetry in your soul, / Is a privilege indeed.'

And so it was with music in his blood and poetry in his soul that Matthew Tuck entered the world on 20 January 1980. His father, who worked for a food company, was a huge fan of music himself, drawn in particular to the quintessential American artists who defined the image of the USA to everyone outside it: the freewheeling literariness of Bob Dylan, the heartland romance of Bob Seger and the blue-collar stargazing of Bruce Springsteen. Matt was the third child of the family, with two older twin sisters, but it was him and his dad who shared the most interests. Their first passion was sport, with Matt pursuing rugby, football, karate and basketball – anything that he could compete in (this determined streak would prove distinctly useful later on). Their second shared passion was, of course, music. His

2

dad would play him records from his favourite singers, and their words, the way in which they would construct their songs, and the cadence of their voices as they sang, all began soaking into the young Tuck's head.

It wasn't a musical education completely devoid of aggression either – Matt's dad was also a fan of Led Zeppelin and he was certainly interested in getting Matt more involved in music. At the age of five, he bought him a full six-piece Premier drum kit and Matt played his very first beats as a musician. As he later told hardDrive Radio, 'I was always being pushed towards music.' And while he didn't necessarily appreciate the influence of his dad's taste in music at the time – what child does? – and has stated that he later got into heavy music as a reaction to his dad's more sedate collection, the influence of those classic songwriters would stay with him long into his adulthood.

However, of Matt's two loves, it was sport that came first. Thanks to an early growth spurt, he was nearly six foot tall by the age of fourteen, which put him at a huge advantage in both basketball and rugby – so much so that he was representing Wales in basketball at that age. But it was also the time that the course of his life would change forever. His parents had recently bought Sky TV, a digital-television service that gave access to hundreds of TV channels, rather than the five terrestrial channels available as standard at the time in the UK. That meant specialist channels and, in particular, MTV: the most influential arbiter of popular music in the days before the Internet. One day Matt was flicking through the channels when a new music clip started. It featured distorted images of a child tossing and turning in bed, cut with strobe shots of fingers on a fretboard and a lingering shot of a skull ring. From the speakers came a riff, languid and cold, yet laced with menace. It was the video for Metallica's 'Enter Sandman' and within ten seconds Matt was hooked. There's no telling how many musicians 'Enter Sandman' has incited to pick up a guitar or sit behind a drum kit for the first time, but in a small market town in South Wales, some three years after its initial release, one teenage boy knew immediately that he wanted to be in a band.

From that point on, Tuck began saving every penny he could. He was consumed by the idea that he would learn to play the guitar and soon he had enough to purchase his first instrument: a white Squier Stratocaster (he would sell it some eighteen months later – a decision he has since come to regret). But with an entry-level electric guitar and a copy of Metallica's self-titled album – the LP that featured 'Enter Sandman', popularly referred to as *The Black Album* – Tuck had everything he needed to begin. He locked himself in his room for hours, days and months on end, determined to learn every riff and lick on the record. Then he moved on to every other Metallica record. He learned the basics of heavy-metal guitar from the band that have been most influential in propagating it; techniques like palm-muting, where the hand is rested on the strings to give a percussive *thud*, and tuning to a lower pitch for a heavier, fatter sound. He had no teacher to show him the ropes or books to guide him; he simply listened to *The Black Album*, over and over, and played until his fingers naturally fell in line with the riffs.

Metallica were not just pioneers of thrash, they were also its figureheads. They have transformed from being merely a band into an institution, backed by a formidable body of work. By combining brutal riffs and fast tempos with an impeccable sense of craft in their songwriting, they eventually became one of the world's most iconic metal bands so, if you wanted to be a musician practising the dark arts of rock, you couldn't go far wrong in using Metallica as your starting point. But crucially, they were also a gateway for Matt, and soon he was devouring a wider range of heavy music, starting with the other players of American thrash metal. There was Slayer, chaotic and savage where Metallica were furiously precise; Anthrax and Megadeth, the two other founding fathers that would, together with Metallica and Slayer, come to be known as the 'Big Four'; and Testament, the Californian act often overlooked for falling outside that quartet of titans.

Beyond thrash metal, Tuck also began listening to more modern American acts and MTV proved to be fertile ground for cultivating his taste. His first experience of Pantera came when he was watching *Headbangers Ball*, a seminal heavy-metal show that ran on MTV from 1987–95. The clip in question was from a live show in Moscow and the song was 'Domination'. Shot in black-and-white, it is not hard to see why it caught his attention. A shirtless Dimebag Darrell tosses his signature mane back and forth like he's having convulsions, while a brutish Phil Anselmo – his head shaven,

'CFH' (*Cowboys From Hell*) tattoo visible – moves around the stage like a man weaving through a crowd at a riot, restless but utterly in control. From Pantera, Tuck moved on to other bands that had taken the thrash template and injected it with a new snarling swagger, like Machine Head (from Oakland, California) and the genre-blurring Sepultura from Brazil. At the same time he also developed an appreciation for the pomp and hedonism of 1980s 'hair metal'. One particular favourite of his was Shotgun Messiah, a Swedish glam metal band whose 1991 album *Second Coming* had all the sex and excess you could want, delivered with a brash punk-rock edge. The key influences that would continue to guide Tuck throughout his career can be found in those acts: brutal American thrash and arena-baiting 1980s metal. As he would later say to German online magazine *DasDing*, 'I always wanted to be in a fuckin' eighties hair metal band anyways. I love that era, I love the style, the attitude, the sex, drugs, rock 'n' roll... but I missed the boat.'

Matt had actually first jammed with friends in school as a drummer but within six months he was already a competent guitar player. At the age of fifteen he sold the drum kit that his dad had bought him to upgrade his guitar gear. He admitted to *Metal Hammer* magazine that he has a tendency to 'geek out' on whatever he gets into, so the time-span between picking up a guitar and being able to play it was shorter than for most and, seeing the progress that he'd made, his parents backed him to the hilt. He has spoken many times of the positive influence his parents have had on his career and the support that they've given him, even when his love of music took the place of his sporting ambitions and, ultimately, his achievements at school ('I went from almost like a semi-professional athlete at a young age and being very focused academically, to being a proper muso pisshead by the time I was sixteen,' he told *Metal Hammer*). With that said, to this day it remains a dream of Matt's to pull on Wales's red jersey just once and have ten minutes representing his country in rugby. It might be an ambition too far.

But no aspiring young musician is going to fulfil his dreams alone, particularly if he's idolising Metallica and Pantera, and Matt was not alone. Since joining his secondary school at the age of eleven – Ogmore School, in the north of the town – he had been hanging out with Michael Thomas. Some people are just destined to get a nickname that more or less replaces their given name and Thomas is one of those people; to future fans, he would always be simply Moose. (He's been somewhat evasive as to the origin of his beastly sobriquet, with explanations offered that include the size of his manhood, his style of making love, or his caveman-like mentality. However, a more sensible suggestion that's been offered is that it's a childhood nickname based on his favourite animal.)

Moose had grown up listening to Queen with his dad – Queen are often credited as one of the progenitors of thrash thanks to their song 'Stone Cold Crazy', so perhaps they had more of an impact on the impressionable Moose than he would later let on. But for him, the band that changed it all was Nirvana. Where grunge can be said to have sprung from the same well as heavy metal, Nirvana's sound had more to do with the noisy art rock of Sonic Youth and the Pixies than the focused rage of Metallica.

Just as Matt was first a drummer, Moose started out as a guitar player. His brother had received a guitar as a Christmas present and from that moment on Moose decided he had to have one too.

He was fourteen years old when he first began playing with Matt but it was when he sat behind a friend's drum kit that he would truly find his feet (in more ways than one). He was a left-hander but his friend's kit was set up right-handed. Instead of switching all the component parts around, he just started playing open-hand style, meaning that he didn't cross his hands to play beats on the snare and hi-hat. 'I was punk rock: I just sat behind my friend's drum kit and picked up the sticks. I didn't know which way it was supposed to go, so that's how I learned,' he explained to *DRUM! Magazine*. He's since expressed regret that he didn't learn to play with the kit set up in the conventional manner that a left-handed drummer would play, as he feels that it's held him back from learning certain techniques, though it's never held back Faith No More's Mike Bordin, Soundgarden/Pearl Jam's Matt Cameron or Tool's Danny Carey.

As a die-hard Nirvana fan, Moose's favourite drummer was, naturally, Dave Grohl, though Matt soon got him hooked on Metallica and he was smashing along with Ulrich to *The Black Album* too. Feeling like his guitar skills were wanting anyway, and getting more and more into the art of drumming thanks to players like Judas Priest's Scott Travis and Slayer's legendary Dave Lombardo (who is often credited for inventing the double-kick drum method), he made the switch to drums. It wasn't the only area where the pair's interests diverged. Where Matt commanded some respect on the rugby pitch, Moose preferred to express his athletic prowess on a skateboard. 'I was always too much of a pussy [to ride skateboards]; I didn't want to bust my face,' Matt told Bullet's official YouTube channel.

But if the pair were going to be in a band, they needed a singer and it was easy to decide who was going to do it. Necessity is the mother of invention, as the saying goes, and only one person they knew was able to play and sing at the same time. 'It just so happened that when I met all the boys and we started getting the music together I was the only one that could really play Metallica riffs and sing at the same time,' Matt told *Metal Hammer*. 'The other guys could play but couldn't do two things at the same time. I was always the kid that could do both.' For almost as long as Matt was playing guitar, he also sang and having to fulfil both responsibilities at the same time would soon become second nature to him.

CHAPTER TWO

SCHOOL OF ROCK

t sixteen, Matt had transitioned fully into what he describes as a 'proper muso pisshead' and headed off to Bridgend College alongside Moose to study a BTEC in music performance. The course had a particularly eccentric leader and one with plenty of experience in the music business himself: Phil Jones, who had formed the band S.E.X. in 1974. Clad in a scarlet cape and wearing a codpiece, together with a bassist who wears nothing at all save his instrument, Jones struts and preens on stage to a soundtrack of synth-inflected, tongue-in-cheek heavy metal. As he put it to *WalesOnline*, 'When The Darkness came along a lot of people said they had stolen my act.' S.E.X. had even scored two chart hits in Australia, with one – entitled 'TV in the UK', which incorporated advert jingles and cartoon theme songs into it

– hitting the top spot in 2000. 'I'm very well placed to teach the students about all the horrible things that might happen to them because I have fallen on my backside in every part of the world,' he observed to *WalesOnline*.

It was at the college, with a course dedicated to music attracting a lot of like-minded young people and with the facilities to help new bands get started, that a real community of budding musicians began to form. There was a group of around twenty students all intermingling in various musical projects across the college and Matt and Moose had been joined by another friend, Nick Crandle, on bass. They took their band name from a saying that had emerged after a classroom prank – someone had stuck a picture of a pornstar named John (most likely John Holmes) onto the wall during a lesson and the teacher – named Jeff – had promptly torn it down. Hence: Jeff Killed John.

However, the band was still looking for another guitar player and they soon found him in a certain Michael Paget – better known as Padge. It was Moose that first introduced him to the rest of Jeff Killed John. They had met while Moose was skateboarding and Padge was walking with a girl, initially striking up a conversation on the simple basis that they shared a name.

It was Nirvana and Metallica, too, that had first made Padge pick up a guitar, with albums being passed around within his friendship group at school, so crossover with the tastes of Matt and Moose was obvious. Later, Padge had also discovered music with a harder edge. 'I came across Pantera and Machine

Head, especially the *Burn My Eyes* album of theirs, and those bands helped me find a new direction which was metal,' he told *Ultimate-Guitar.com* website. However, Padge's tastes extended beyond buzzsaw riffs and frantic drums; he was also a huge fan of the blues and, in particular, Stevie Ray Vaughan. Vaughan hit the heights in the 1980s, almost single-handedly bringing about a revival in the popularity of the blues, while injecting his playing with flavours of legendary guitar players from across the jazz and rock 'n' roll spectrum: in particular that of Jimi Hendrix. The result was the grit of the blues approached with a near virtuosic level of ability, and for two years Padge practically lived and breathed the blues. Still, he found that heavy metal was his enduring love: 'I still love rock and blues but metal has got, and always will [have], a bit more edge for me,' he told *Ultimate-Guitar.com*.

In fact, it was from Padge that Moose had bought his first drum kit, upon deciding that he was not destined to be a guitar player. Matt and Moose started playing covers – mostly Nirvana and Metallica songs but also oddities from Chumba Wumba or tunes from local heroes like Stereophonics – but quickly moved on to writing their own material, and it wasn't long before they had made a couple of original songs together. So Padge headed over to Matt's house and learned the guitar lines. They may not have been the most sophisticated songs but it was still original material, which is what counted. In fact, one of the first songs Padge learned with the lads, entitled 'Wrong of Me', would later show up on Jeff Killed John's first EP.

For Matt, it was the community of musicians that was the most useful aspect of attending Bridgend College, rather than the actual course itself. 'It was the first year that this college had the course going, they didn't even have a computer in the class, all we did was go there, jam and get drunk; it was just a crazy band house rather than a college,' Matt would later comment to the *BlairingOut.com* YouTube channel. 'All of us went there 'cause all we wanted to do was music... but it was nothing anyways. Apparently now it's a really good course, but when we did it it was a bunch of guys jamming out, getting drunk, and trying to pull girls.' Their education, ultimately, was to come from getting out into the world and experiencing it for themselves, first-hand.

Jeff Killed John first appeared on record on a compilation entitled *Allsorts!* The first track contributed is called 'Bouncy Stuff', which skips along on a suitably spongy riff and has Matt channelling Zack de la Rocha at one point with an exclamation of 'bring that shit!' The second offering, 'Hostile', is a more punk-rock affair with largely unintelligible lyrics and a rudimentary riff. There's little on display to hint at the band that they would later become.

Not long after Padge joined Jeff Killed John, the band headed to the studio to record their first EP, which was released in 1999 after the band had left Bridgend College. Entitled *Better Off Alone*, it shows a band clearly possessed of songwriting nous and proficient on their instruments but, stylistically, it is very much a product of its era. Despite almost all of Bullet's key influences coming from either the

New Wave of British Heavy Metal (N.W.O.B.H.M.) – such as Iron Maiden and Judas Priest – or the American thrash-metal movement, which included Metallica, Slayer and, later, Pantera, the late 1990s was very much the reign of 'nu metal', with bands such as Korn, Limp Bizkit and Papa Roach making big waves on the live circuit and appealing to a new, younger audience with their fusion of styles. In 1998 Korn's third album *Follow the Leader* had made it to the top of American album chart the Billboard 200, signalling that this new iteration of heavy metal was now big business. It was shortly followed by the likes of Deftones' *Around the Fur*, Slipknot's self-titled debut and Limp Bizkit's *Significant Other* (which also peaked at number one on the Billboard 200).

In truth, the nu-metal tag was a broad descriptor used to lump together a whole new wave of American bands that, in many cases, had only passing similarities with one another. Sure, Slipknot's debut featured scratching and a brief burst of pseudo-rapping but its thick, quasi-industrial and menacingly heavy sound had little else to do with hip-hop. Limp Bizkit, on the other hand, used live instrumentation to mimic hip-hop beats and fused these with big rock choruses. Deftones had the atmosphere and romanticism of a British new-wave band, in complete contrast to the violence and nihilism of other bands in the so-called movement. But nonetheless, the genre had its defining elements – most notably simple, repetitive, detuned riffs, a world away from the fiddly guitar heroics of classic heavy metal. And Jeff Killed John's *Better Off Alone* EP has these in spades.

The title track, which also opens the EP, for example, begins with a one-bar syncopated bass riff that is soon mirrored by the guitars, and the warbling tremolo guitar effect in the verse could be heard on any number of Korn songs. But even at this early stage, Matt possesses a commanding vocal style and Moose's drumming displays plenty of the controlled power he would later be known for. 'Bottom of the Line' uses the same trick: a pummelling guitar riff to kick things off, a variation of the riff to carry the verse and a return of the riff for the chorus. Structurally, it's incredibly simple but the song is not without character. The verse has the playful bounce of System of a Down, an influence that can also be heard in the frantic bass playing but the vocal effect saturating Matt's voice in the chorus showcases just how good the band already were at knowing how to create a memorable hook in an unrelentingly heavy song.

They were also experimenting with different tempos and formats at this time, as demonstrated by 'Wrong of Me', one of the first two songs that Matt taught Padge when he joined Jeff Killed John. And as a very early composition, it's interesting to hear that this has a more generic indie-rock chorus, with little in common with the harder material on offer elsewhere on *Better Off Alone*. It was the first time that any of the boys had heard Padge play a solo and the song is peppered with melodramatic leads that show plenty of awareness of how to write a melodic guitar line, while not displaying any of the highly technical sweeps and speed runs that he would later be known for. Padge's analysis of his fretwork, however, is less forgiving; speaking to Dutch online magazine *FaceCulture* many years later, he would simply refer to this first recorded solo as 'fucking terrible'.

The four-track release closes with 'Don't Walk Away', which takes us back into nu-metal territory and the detuned, repeated power-chord riff. The vocal line in the verse of 'Don't Walk Away' has, perhaps, more in common with punk, and the call-and-response of the chorus is pure masculine angst, but it can't be denied that there's a pop sensibility at work here. It's also the first time that we hear the band utilise vocal harmonies effectively, which would later become a key weapon in Tuck's arsenal. The song closes with a rip-roaring solo, very much out of vogue among the nu-metal crowd and showing that the boys weren't quite ready to write off their classic-metal influences. The seeds of Bullet for My Valentine were undoubtedly there; they were just very much buried.

CHAPTER THREE

'THE NEW SEATTLE'

With Jeff Killed John clearly under the influence of the new breed of American metal acts that had emerged towards the end of the twenty-first century, Bridgend probably felt like it was a very long way from the action indeed. As Matt put it himself, it was just a normal Welsh town where everyone seemed to know everyone else's business. But as the millennium hit, the fact was that, to the rest of the UK and beyond, South Wales was starting to look quite special.

For a long time Welsh pop music was synonymous with one man: the baritone-voiced, carpet-chested lothario of the valleys, Tom Jones. But in the mid to late 1990s Wales had well and truly been put on the alternative-music map by Manic Street Preachers. They were the ultimate pop provocateurs. Their lyrics could be political and confessional, sometimes they dressed in women's blouses and sometimes in balaclavas, and they pulled influences from many different genres into their restless and infinitely inventive albums. By the time their third album, *The Holy Bible*, was released, they were regarded by many as one of the most interesting guitar bands in the UK. In short, they were exactly the band that Wales needed. Other acts followed – most notably Stereophonics, Catatonia and Super Furry Animals, the so-called 'Cool Cymru' set – but for most of the 1990s the Manics remained the quintessential Welsh guitar band, particularly after the critical and commercial smash of their fourth record, *Everything Must Go*.

As the new millennium loomed no one was particularly expecting Wales to deliver on the 'Next Big Thing' but a young band from Pontypridd nominated themselves for the role anyway. Lostprophets began life as a side project to hardcore band Public Disturbance and went through a period of line-up changes and small-scale tours as they independently released three EPs. They were regulars on the South Wales circuit, which had a number of venues of the right size and with the right attitude to showcase new talent: Clwb Ifor Bach and The Barfly in Cardiff, The Toll House in Bridgend and TJ's in Newport. The latter, in particular, is an iconic venue with enough lore attached to it to fill a book in its own right and is, supposedly, the venue where Kurt Cobain proposed to Courtney Love after Hole played there in 1991.

Eventually, Lostprophets signed to independent rock

label Visible Noise and recorded their debut album, *Thefakesoundofprogress*, in under two weeks and for a few thousand pounds. It was rough and ready, made up, at least in part, of reworked demos but, with its sly combination of American post-hardcore, nu metal, and pop-culture references, they caught the attention of the public. The success of first single 'Shinobi vs. Dragon Ninja' was enough to convince Columbia Records to sign the band, who re-recorded and re-released their debut. Suddenly, the band were blowing up in America as well as the UK and a lot of eyes were on South Wales to see if there was more where that came from.

There were a number of other bands drawing from American post-hardcore influences around South Wales at that time, like Hondo Maclean – a noise-mongering outfit whose style bordered on technical metalcore – The Blackout from Merthyr Tydfil, who wove a pop-punk influence into the sound, and Midasuno, also from Merthyr. Ammanford's Jarcrew had a more eclectic approach, mixing post-punk and progressive-rock influences together into a kind of jagged, dance-floor-baiting take on Gang of Four, whereas Cardiff's Mclusky were the veteran bruisers of the scene – a power trio with a keen sense of humour and an ear for a thrillingly dissonant racket. The previous incarnation of The Automatic, who would come to mainstream prominence in 2006, were also on the scene, performing under the name White Rabbit. The bands were not necessarily all associated and the different bands' sounds were incredibly varied but it was, nonetheless, an incredibly fertile scene with the venues to support it. The existence of Mighty Atom Records in Swansea, which also boasted its own recording facilities, added to the health of the scene.

However, it was Funeral for a Friend who would prove to be next out of the gate and go on to mainstream success. Like Jeff Killed John, they were from Bridgend, with singer Matthew Davies (now Davies-Kreye) having met the rest of the band through working at The Jungle record store in the town and through connections at school and college. Funeral for a Friend began as a metalcore act called January Thirst but the addition of Davies-Kreye added a melodic vocal approach to the brutal guitar work, and the band slowly began to seamlessly blend the brute force of hardcore with the open-hearted pop sensibilities of emo.

They signed to Mighty Atom Records, where they had also been recording, and released their debut EP *Between Order and Model* in 2002. It was shortly followed by tours with US bands Boysetsfire and The Juliana Theory, who were heading over to the UK for the first time. One of the most interesting things about Funeral for a Friend was that they were taking fundamentally American styles and merging them with a distinctly regional sensibility, as Davies-Kreye told *Rock Sound* magazine: 'There were no other bands in the UK doing what we were so we felt as if we were part of an American scene to a degree. We felt more of a kinship to a lot of American bands than we did [to] anything that was going on in the UK at that point.'

After winning a Kerrang! Award for Best British Newcomer in 2003, Funeral for a Friend released their debut album, *Casually Dressed & Deep in Conversation*, in October, through Atlantic Records. It was an immediate hit with the music critics and produced three top-twenty singles in the UK. By 2004 the band were off on tour around the USA with Linkin Park. At the same time, Lostprophets had continued to grow in renown thanks to the release of their second album, *Start Something*, which had a more tepid critical response than their debut but which was, nonetheless, commercially successful in both the US and the UK. Two bands from two small mining communities in a country of three million, with little to superficially connect them other than a decades-old sporting rivalry, were tearing up the charts across the English-speaking world. There had to be more to it than chance.

It's not exactly clear who first dubbed South Wales 'The New Seattle', after the American city synonymous with the grunge movement in the 1990s, though it was most likely popularised by *Spin* magazine after they used the phrase to title an article about Newport's TJ's. But whatever the cause of the major-label feeding frenzy that descended on South Wales following the success of Lostprophets and Funeral for a Friend, for Matthew Davies-Kreye, the tag was not justified. In an illuminating article for online music mag *Noisey.Vice.com* called SOUTH WALES WAS THE NEW SEATTLE? TOTAL BOLLOCKS, he writes, 'They were nothing alike other than the fact that we're by the coast, it's depressing, and it rains for 290 of the days of the year.'

However, he does give an incredible account of the South Wales music scene in the early 2000s before it came to the nation's attention. He states his view that the venues were incredibly important, particularly because they would often host pop-up record stores: 'Even if I wasn't too familiar with the band playing,' he writes, 'I'd go to shows knowing my friends were going to be there… It was a very honest, pure environment to be in.' Davies-Kreye also pays tribute to the diversity of the scene, which would often see bands from completely different genres hosted on the same bill, with an atmosphere of mutual support throughout. 'You'd have hardcore kids, punk kids, nu-metal kids, hip-hop kids, nobody really knew what they were and it didn't matter,' he explains in the piece. 'It was a mash-up of people and influences, which made being a part of it quite beautiful. There were no boundaries, most people were just really passionate about the fact that local bands were writing their own songs that were actually good.'

CHAPTER FOUR

I HEAR YOU'RE IN A BAND

Jeff Killed John found themselves in the midst of this excitement around the thriving South Wales scene, continuing to rehearse and play gigs while working at menial day jobs to support themselves. Padge had, at one point, been working bending metal and, at another, hammering the wire frame into dartboards. One of Moose's first jobs was in a pet store. Matt was putting in hours in a local Virgin XS, an arm of Virgin Megastore set up to sell off back-catalogue stock. It was here that he met one particular naysayer who stuck in his mind. 'Once, a regional manager came down and he was like, "I hear you're in a band," and asked about it,' he related to *Metal Hammer*. 'So I told him and he was just a total dick. Like, "I'd just give it up now. What do you do? Metal? You're never gonna get signed..." He just took the piss so much. Shit like that, for me, that's like ammunition to prove myself even more.'

Fortunately, his parents continued to support him through his younger years, recognising that he had committed himself to achieving success. 'They'd drive me to practice and buy me new equipment whenever I needed it, like upgrades to bigger and better things,' he told *Reverb Street Press* magazine (now *Reverb Online*). 'They even paid for studio time so we could do demos. They're just amazing parents and I couldn't have asked anything more of them. They did exactly what they needed to do because I had a dream, you know. I'll be forever thankful for it.'

However, by 2002 they were finding other means of funding their growth. A corporate communications company had secured some £500,000 of funding from the European Union for a scheme called Promoting Youth Networks in the Cultural Industries, or PYNCI. The money was earmarked specifically to help young musicians in the area and Jeff Killed John were one of the bands selected for funding over the two years that the scheme ran. They used it to head into the studio with Greg Haver, a producer who had been heavily involved with the Manic Street Preachers since the release of their 1998 album *This Is My Truth Tell Me Yours*. He had also worked extensively with another stalwart of the Welsh scene, Skindred, a Newport-based band that fused the anger of punk and metal with the energy of dub and ragga.

The outcome of Jeff Killed John's collaboration with Greg Haver was a two-track release and by far the strongest material that the band had laid down to date. The first song, 'You', shows a clear leap in ability from previous recordings. Moose has got a real handle on the double-kick pedal, with his rapid footwork matching the crunching riffs, and the chorus combines screamed vocals with harmonised singing in one undeniably effective hook. Musically, it's still a maelstrom of relatively unsophisticated power-chord riffing and the half-rapped, half-screamed breakdown that brings the track to an end is pure nu metal, but there's no denying that they had sharpened both their songwriting skills and their playing since the *Better Off Alone* EP.

It's accompanied by 'Phony', a track sometimes listed as 'Play With Me'. The riffs are tightly wound but delivered with nuance, and the screaming section that follows each chorus ('Come play with me / 'cause I am lonely / why can't you see / that you're a phony') demonstrates that the band has some real fire in its belly, with Moose once again wailing on the double kick. The band had started to let a little bit more of their classic-metal influence creep in and as a result, 'Phony' was their strongest song to date. On one release the two tracks were also packaged with a cover of the Phil Collins' classic 'In the Air Tonight', which the band were also covering live around this time. With heavily processed drums and vocals and stabs of distorted chords that drift across the clean guitar lines like toxic ash, it has an almost industrial feel, heightened when the song kicks off at the three-quarter mark.

Just as the band had made strides in the quality of their

recorded output, they were building a real name for themselves locally too. One key figure in supporting Jeff Killed John and a whole host of other acts on the South Wales scene was Glyn Mills, a man with the natural flow of a raconteur and an infectious cackle. Mills had first become involved in the scene while working for an organisation based in South Wales aimed at helping young people and had discovered that music was an extremely important outlet for a lot of the teenagers in the area. 'We found from talking to the young people that music was the key thing, especially with disaffected kids,' he explains. 'Some were very disaffected, but they just needed a bit of attention.' Mills had been working on various projects to provide facilities in the area, including raising £125,000 for a skatepark, so it made sense to provide them with a platform to play music as well. As such, he started putting on local gigs in youth centres around the area.

Mills was also reviewing for local publications at the time and had first written about Jeff Killed John at a show in 2002 at Clwb Ifor Bach in Cardiff, where they were supporting the Newport-based band Douglas. What's fascinating about the review is how many of the elements that would later come to define Bullet for My Valentine were already present here, years before Bullet existed. He talks of how aggressively Moose plays the drums, of how far Padge's playing contrasts with his laid-back character. In a rare account of Nick Crandle's contribution, he speaks of his 'mesmerising [...] menacing and sinister' stage persona, and Matt gets lauded not just for how far his voice has developed but also for the attention he gets from the female members of the audience. The review concludes, 'They used to play like they had something to prove, now they play like they've already proved it.'

Mills had already linked up with Bridgend College, who recognised that the assistance of a promoter for the local scene would be instrumental in helping students on the Music Performance course get real-world experience. 'When [the college] heard that we were putting on gigs – obviously they had young lads, and they would say, "Can you help put this band on?"' Mills explains (Jeff Killed John had already moved on from Bridgend College at this point). 'It worked from there, and Jeff Killed John were building their reputation, so they got to know about us.' Like most things, social circles were a crucial means of building new relationships too and Mills had also come to know of Moose through his brother Shiner, who was playing guitar in a local band named Then Came Bronson. (Shiner would later sign to Visible Noise with another band, Miss Conduct, featuring two other members of Then Came Bronson. There's clearly something special in the Thomas genes.)

One of the early venues Mills used to host gigs was the Brackla Community Centre, in the east of the town. During wartime, Brackla had been home to the largest factory in western Europe and, as fighting ended, the land was sold to developers. They used the site to construct one of Europe's largest privately owned housing estates and some five decades later it was not the din of munitions manufacture ringing through the air but the noise of young rock and metal bands. Then Came Bronson had been regular performers at the stage and, about six months into the run, Jeff Killed John headlined a show at the Brackla. The nights would inevitably get a little rowdy and the crowds were getting bigger and bigger, with many turning up to see Jeff Killed John specifically.

Playing before Jeff Killed John on that night was a band called Nuke. They were also from Bridgend College and Glyn Mills was managing them. Their guitar player, Jamie Hanford, was studying for a sound-tech qualification and would go on to do live sound for Jeff Killed John many times in the future while working for a South Wales promotions company. 'The "scene" was thriving back in the early 2000s,' Hanford recalls of the period. 'I was a sound engineer for a local promotions company and would normally work five or six nights a week right across south-east Wales. So many names from all over the world would play a fantastic mix of music; it wasn't just rock and metal.'

And it was the second time that night that a local bass player and vocalist called Jason James, better known as Jay, had taken the stage. He had first appeared with Endurone, though he was not officially their singer and was only filling in until they found a suitable replacement (Endurone also featured Glyn Mills's son on drums). But his main role was in Nuke. Like most, Jay had got his first taste of music through the elders in his house, with his father a devotee of classic rock 'n' roll – Elvis Presley in particular – and his brother a big fan of Queen. But when he was twelve, he had bought a tape from his friend for a fiver that would irrevocably change his life. It was *Appetite for Destruction* by Guns N' Roses and it made an immediate impression on the innocent young mind. 'When I took it home and put it on, I just could not believe what I was listening to, you know what I mean,' Jay told *Spotlight Report*. 'It was heavy and there was swearing in there, and I was like "oh my God, what the hell is this?"'

Matt Tuck had also had a part to play in Jay's musical education. Jay, being a couple of years Tuck's junior, was a friend of Matt's younger cousin. One day, while Jay was visiting, Matt appeared with a stack of Metallica albums for the pair to listen to. From there, it was heavy metal all the way for Jay, with Pantera and Slayer following quickly after Metallica. Iron Maiden's Steve Harris first inspired Jay to pick up a bass guitar and provided the basic teachings, and he joined Nuke at the age of fifteen.

Nuke and Jeff Killed John were very close from within the community – they even used the same rehearsal space – and had developed something of a friendly rivalry with one another. Speaking about the scene in general, Mills is keen to point out how bands were supportive of one another. 'There was always a friendly rivalry. People would talk about who's better, particular fans had particular favourites, but it was never underhanded; people used to help one another out,' he says. 'If you went to a party it would all be the same boys, and you'd find them supporting each other, going to one another's gigs, etc.'

The night that Nuke and Jeff Killed John appeared

after one another would turn out to be the last gig Brackla Community Centre hosted. 'It got so, so full, there were literally hundreds of kids turned up,' Mills recalls. 'The audience ruined the floor, a highly polished floor, they couldn't use it for a week... I think the cans of beer on the newly polished floor were not appreciated.' But it would take more than a sticky floor at a community centre to stop the ever-growing pace of the South Wales scene. Mills moved on to be the in-house promoter at local venue the Toll House, previously known as Jaggers, becoming a key figure in the Bridgend scene alongside his friend Darren Dobbs. 'They asked us if we wanted to take on the Toll House, and I was ex-marketing, and thought, "Well there can't be that much to it."' he recalls. 'I said I'd give it three months and in the end I was there for years.'

Under Mills's guidance, both local bands and those from further afield were increasingly keen to come to Bridgend. 'We were booking bands left, right, and centre. Bands were coming to us, it was a real good scene,' he says. 'There were times when we were actually turning people away because there were so many people turning up. We were disappointed if there was less than a three-figure number in; we used to wonder what we'd done wrong.'

A more difficult question to answer is exactly what factors were in play in South Wales at the time that there should have been so many notable bands coming up in such a small area, in towns with relatively small populations. For Mills, it's impossible to ignore the economic considerations. 'It was new music that was coming through; guys were looking for an alternative lifestyle and a way to express themselves, 'cos there was a lot of social issues going on in the valleys at the time,' he explains. 'You're talking about the late nineties, early noughties when there was a tremendous amount of change. We'd lost employment, we'd lost the mines, we'd lost steelworks, everything had gone. And in place of it were jobs that were minimum wage. There was very little to offer at the time, and there still isn't to a certain degree.'

However, it was not the promise of wealth and riches per se that got people into bands; it was merely the desire to be acknowledged for whatever ability they did have. 'Years ago, the saying was you either went down the mines or you went into teaching. To get out of Wales you had to go teaching. Well, I guess being a musician kind of replaced that.' As more and more people started to find their way into bands, it had a snowballing effect of pulling more and more young people into the scene. As Mills puts it, 'people were feeding off one another.'

And while Matt felt that his time at Bridgend College was not particularly helpful, for Jamie Hanford, formerly of Nuke, the college did provide important facilities to get people started. 'We were all students at Bridgend College at a time when the arts were funded by the government, so everyone had space and instruments to use,' he points out. 'So it was just natural and a part of our diplomas to jam. [It] was a really exciting, fun time.'

As things developed, Mills was putting on more and more

gigs, ultimately hosting two per week in Bridgend and one a week in Cardiff, as well as the occasional show in London. 'Suddenly, South Wales became the epicentre of everybody's activity because there was a realisation that we had a scene going on down here that wasn't affected by London,' Mills explains; Jeff Killed John, too, were regularly leaving Wales and heading to London to help get their name out beyond their local area. Momentum was building and, from the outside looking in, it seemed as if Jeff Killed John couldn't have been in a better place at a better time to get signed. But they were about to encounter a serious hurdle.

CHAPTER FIVE

DEPARTURES

The band were only to complete one final EP as Jeff Killed John and this time the roots of the band that they would become were absolutely undeniable. The self-titled release from 2003 features a whole range of melodies and lyrics that would later show up on Bullet for My Valentine's debut EP and album, though in a much altered form. It opens with 'Our Song', a number with a crushing chorus and plenty of athletic drum fills from Moose, as well as an atmospheric breakdown with a creeping groove, though it's not a huge step forward from the material that they recorded with Greg Haver.

The next track, however – called 'Routine Unhappiness' – showed that they were really getting to grips with the mechanics of writing a catchy rock song. Pivoting on an off-kilter riff, the vocals are pushed right to the front of the mix and Matt pulls out every trick in the book in his performance to sell the sordid tale of domestic abuse to the listener, with his gutsy singing line breaking into a scream at various points. The guitar work is held back to give space for the singing to properly take centre stage and the song's middle eight lifts off with a wordless refrain of 'whoah-ohs'. Even in this most raw format, it sounds as if it's destined to be played in rooms larger than a community centre. It's rough and unpolished but there's no doubt that the boys were starting to feel and sound like a band with big ambitions.

The third track, 'Nation2Nation', features a guest appearance from a certain Benji Webbe – the vocalist of Skindred. The band had been formed in Newport in 1998 after Webbe's previous project, Dub War, had languished on Earache Records, forcing him to reconfigure the line-up and start a new project. Their debut album, *Babylon*, was released in 2002 to a positive reception, with critics praising the release for its fresh and unfiltered take on metal – in addition to the blazing riffs and pneumatic drums you'd expect from a solid heavy album, *Babylon* incorporated a bold streak of reggae and dancehall, with Webbe's highly versatile and distinctive vocal the focus of their hybrid approach. Webbe had first fallen in love with both punk rock and reggae at school (when his friends were all announcing their allegiance to this tribe or that with their dress sense, he just wanted dreadlocks with a mohawk in the middle, he told online fansite *Metal as Fuck*). It's a testament to his support for the scene that, despite being an RCA-signed artist at this time, he was still helping out unsigned acts in the area and his work with up-and-coming Welsh acts continues to this date, in addition to regularly touring with Skindred.

'Nation2Nation' opens with the sound of a siren, a sample heavily used in dancehall, before a cyclical riff kicks in. The verse sees Matt incorporating another nu-metal rap, as on 'You' – it's a product of the era that the EP was produced in but it's pulled off with gusto nonetheless. The chorus is pure vitriol, with traded screams pinging back and forth over the driving riff, and Webbe appears in the second verse, stealing the show somewhat with an elastic vocal line combining death-metal growls with the rhythms and inflections of Jamaica. It's a fascinating experiment in playing with the Jeff Killed John style that, despite not having a lot in common with JKJ's future approach, does show that the band were more than prepared to explore unfamiliar territory with their music – a trait that would last throughout their career.

The track is important in the Bullet for My Valentine story for another, less apparent reason. Skindred signed to RCA Records and released *Babylon* in July 2002 but in November of that year two of its founding members had left – the drummer, Martyn Ford (better known as 'Ginge') and guitarist Jeff Rose (also known as Jeff 'Death' Rose). In detailed joint statements, Ford in particular cited mistreatment at the hands of RCA, writing, 'After recording our stunning album *Babylon* and doing some amazing shows seeing the reaction from people to our music I knew we deserved to be treated much better than the way we had been by RCA, the label total [sic] didn't push the band or the album in the way a major label can when they believe in it.' Both members instead decided to pursue a career in recording. Ford had set up a makeshift studio beneath a boxing gym in Newport to track the demos for Skindred's debut and, experiencing Pro Tools (a digital audio workstation) for the first time after recording *Babylon* in Hollywood, he saw his future. Upon leaving Skindred, he decided to found his own recording studio. The result was Not In Pill, in Newport, and the first band to record there were Jeff Killed John. It was the start of a longstanding creative collaboration that would last throughout Bullet for My Valentine's career (Ford would also go on to work with Slipknot, Trivium, As I Lay Dying and many more).

Around this time Jeff Killed John had also recorded a track that will be familiar to all and it is another example of how far they had developed in the craft of writing songs. Opening with a simple acoustic-guitar part accompanied by a vocal, 'All These Things I Hate (Revolve Around Me)' shows a band that know how to structure a composition, with each vocal line carefully designed to stick in the listener's head and with the lyrics clearly audible. While the drumming and guitar work is still prominent, it's in service to the emotional tone of the song. Matt was developing as a lyricist too and had the smarts to write songs around highly relatable themes, such as the collapse of a relationship.

But if Jeff Killed John were experimenting with a more accessible and approachable take on their sound at this time, they weren't about to go full pop, as the next track on the EP demonstrates. Entitled 'Misery', it opens with an extended instrumental section, a pensive guitar line underpinned by a spartan drum part from Moose, which also forms the basis for the melancholic verse. But all hell breaks loose in the chorus, which also shows just how strong a scream Matt could pull out at this time.

While the *Jeff Killed John* EP shows that the band were, if not ready to blow, at least making significant strides, the truth was that all was not well around the period that this EP was recorded. Although South Wales was well and truly under scrutiny from the industry, all the increased pressure was causing some discontent in the Jeff Killed John ranks. They were broke and in debt. Outside of the nurturing scene within Wales, they were regularly getting involved in pay-to-play shows, whereby bands have to pay some sort of fee upfront to the promoter to get on the bill, usually with the promise of compensation if enough punters come through the door. Their commitment to the band had seen all of them, at one time or another, lose a job.

Plus, seeing other local bands get snapped up by majors was causing something of a crisis of confidence. 'We just kept thinking "what are we doing wrong?"' Padge revealed to *Ultimate Guitar*. 'All these bands were getting signed up and we'd been going just as long, if not longer than some of those bands and we couldn't figure it out.' Things were about to get worse. The band was gearing up to enter the studio but bassist Nick Crandle decided he had had enough.

'We were due to go in the studio on Saturday, and he quit on the Friday,' Matt told *The Gauntlet* website. 'Everything went completely tits up.'

CHAPTER SIX

LOOK AT ME NOW

The band entered a period of soul-searching. They had already dedicated years to Jeff Killed John and, despite coming close on a number of occasions, they had watched other bands in the area break out of the local scene while they remained in relative obscurity. Now they were down a member too.

With nothing left to lose, the band took stock of everything that they had built up so far and decided to change the direction they had been heading in. Moose explained it to the Voice of Rock Radio like this: 'We'd had eight years of jumping on bandwagons, and being kids, we didn't know our identity as musicians, and we were jumping from bandwagon to bandwagon. It wasn't working, so we thought, let's analyse why it's not working, and we tried to make music that sums up all our influences on one song.'

That song came along while the band were practising in the dilapidated old church where they used to rehearse. Where they had previously followed the nu-metal template of dense, power-chord based riffs, usually a bar in length and repeated over and over, they started to look more to the bands that they had been most influenced by when they were growing up; the classic thrash and heavy metal that had first made them want to pick up an instrument and play. One thing that stood out as notably different to what they were doing was the guitar work. It could be thick and blunt but it could also be intricate, almost baroque, with twin guitar lines playing contrapuntal melodies or reflecting one another in harmonised lines. Once the decision had been made to call time on the nu-metal style that the band had been pursuing – and weren't really interested in as fans anymore anyway – the harmonised twin-guitar approach naturally started to express itself in their songwriting. The result was '4 Words to Choke Upon', a song that not only absorbed and modernised a whole host of classic-metal influences but also managed to stick the middle finger up lyrically to everyone who said Jeff Killed John would never make it.

The song felt like a catalyst for something. They had hit on a rich vein of material and there was no telling how deep the mine went. They began writing furiously but, rather than trying to force themselves into a certain mould, they just allowed the songs to come out organically. 'There was no specific decision made,' Matt told *RoomThirteen*. 'We just started to write and whatever happened, happened. Luckily it totally worked [...] The harmony guitars and big angelic choruses seemed to have just progressed from there.'

At this time the band were also looking for a replacement for Nick and, fortunately, they were in the midst of a scene teeming with musicians. One candidate was even from Ogmore Vale, the same village as where Jeff Killed John came from. It was Jason James, the bass player for Nuke, who they had shared a stage with many times over. However, the decision to leave behind Nuke was not an easy one for James. Glyn Mills, who had been managing Nuke, remembers it like this: 'It got to the point when Nick left – I'm not sure quite what happened there – but they were looking for a new bassist. They approached Jay, and Jay was in Nuke at the time. I met Jay in town and he was beside himself not knowing what to do, 'cos they were his best mates in Nuke – they'd grown up together. But my advice to him was, look, if they're friends, they'll understand. You can't turn that opportunity down. But they all stayed pretty close in the end, obviously first of all there was bother but they're all good friends.'

As it happens, for a time, Nick Crandle actually joined Nuke, who started going by the name Emily All Over. Nick Crandle has since left but the core of the band – Jamie Hanford, Rob Norris and Sion Woodbine – are still playing today. As Hanford explains, 'We needed to change the name of the band so we could start fresh and give us all equal ownership of our music (in terms of putting an end point to

Nuke). That's when we became As Silence Falls.' In 2013 As Silence Falls released a self-titled five-track EP of technical, ferocious metalcore combined with emotive, melodic vocals. Recorded by none other than Martyn Ford and Jeff Rose at Not in Pill Studios and the recipient of a 4K review in *Kerrang!*, they have added their name to the already extensive list of great rock bands from South Wales.

With Jay in the ranks, the sense of the band being on the right track was heightened even more, as Matt would later relate in an interview with Scuzz TV. 'As soon as Jay came in, it felt different – it felt weird, and it felt right,' he said. 'We weren't aware of what was happening, and looking back at the early gigs we did, they weren't in my opinion all that great – but there was something about us four guys doing something at that time that felt a bit different.' It was only natural that the band sought to rebrand themselves. They didn't like the name Jeff Killed John anyway – after all, it was a name they had picked for themselves when they were teenagers – and for a time they had been going by the name Opportunity in Chicago. Deciding that wasn't quite right either, a brainstorming session was in order and, naturally, it happened down the pub. Armed with a pen, a sheet of paper and a pint each, the band started throwing out potentials. It was Moose who first came up with 'Violence for My Valentine' but it was deemed too death metal. So the band drew from some songs that they had at the time and settled on 'Bullet for My Valentine'. It had the right juxtaposition of sweetness and savagery, which also seemed to reflect the more melodic take on metal that they were putting together.

With their aspirations up and running again, Bullet for My Valentine started rehearsing hard. And instead of plying their new sound and identity locally, they were going to head to London to get in front of people who they knew had the power to offer them contracts. They had come close before but never quite got there, as Glyn Mills recalls: 'They were on the tips of the tongues of everyone as being the band that were gonna get signed, and there were a couple of times that they thought this was it. There were a few disappointments on the way.' This was to be the last push.

The band had already acquired management through a demo they had sent to the Camden Barfly and, in February of 2004, Bullet for My Valentine were booked on a showcase in London in front of a number of labels. It was only their second show under the name but, after near to a decade of no success with Jeff Killed John, the response was immediate. There was not one but two labels vying for the band's signatures.

The first was Roadrunner Records, a legendary metal imprint that had released albums from King Diamond, Machine Head, Sepultura, Type O Negative, Opeth and Slipknot, among many others. Roadrunner Records had the pedigree; it was a dedicated rock-and-metal label that had broken a number of highly influential acts and had proven itself time and time again to be ahead of the curve when it came to signing genre-defining acts. But the other label was Sony Music Entertainment, the second largest music company in the world (after Universal Music Group). They had clout, cash and literally hundreds of artists on their roster, from pretty much every genre imaginable. And they had globally renowned rock acts, everything from Foo Fighters to Ozzy Osbourne, Slayer and the mighty Iron Maiden (in the UK).

Bullet for My Valentine were in a quandary. It was a nice problem to have but, after having waited so long to get to here, there was a huge amount of pressure to get this decision right. Roadrunner Records was, by all accounts, the obvious choice because of the legacy that they had in working with new metal acts. But the band were concerned about the longevity of the bands on their roster. 'Roadrunner is a great label, they have great artists, but we feel that after album number two, nothing much happens,' Moose told *InTheNews*. 'The bands kind of fall off the face of the Earth.' Having worked so hard to get to this point, the boys had every intention of becoming the biggest band that they could possibly be, they wanted to surpass every expectation. The Sony deal was stronger financially and the band felt that it would offer them more longevity. As Matt put it to *Metal Hammer*, '[We thought], "let's step out of the metal comfort zone and stand head and shoulders above everyone else that we come across."' And so the band finally agreed a five-album deal with Sony.

With the ink barely dry on the contract, they immediately set about the first order of business: celebrating, in the most rock 'n' roll sense imaginable. They hit London hard, racking up a tab on Sony's card at a plethora of bars and, later, a strip club. After the festivities they headed back to a hotel that the label had put on for them. Bullet for My Valentine were now a signed band; they were professional musicians. There was only one thing to do – trash the room. A sofa went through the wall and into the next room. The TV wouldn't fit out the window, so they threw it on the floor and pissed on it instead.

It was the culmination of everything that the band had worked for up to this point; they had kept going, well past the point it would have been sensible to give up, until they simply could not be ignored anymore. But the truth is that Bullet for My Valentine were also, in another sense, incredibly lucky. For a start, Matt himself has acknowledged that, were the band to have been signed five years prior, when they were still very much in the midst of their nu-metal phase, they probably would have fallen out of favour and been dropped before 2004 even came along.

And secondly, in 2004 the music business was on the cusp of a huge schism. Peer-to-peer downloading had already become a major channel for the exchange of music; in 2003 iTunes started offering legal downloads and in 2007 the Internet became the biggest channel in the world for the exchange of music, though the revenue made from legal downloads nowhere near made up for the loss of revenue from traditional media. The result was that the kind of major-label, multi-album contracts that Bullet for My Valentine were offered dwindled in availability. These days, the climate for bands is considerably more inhospitable, with many having to sign away all kinds of rights to get any backing at all.

But all of that was irrelevant in 2004; all that mattered was that the chase was over. Matt put it best to *The Aquarian Weekly* newspaper: 'Getting a record deal is the biggest achievement and highlight of our life,' he said. 'Not even of our career, but our life. We worked so hard to accomplish [this] with no guarantee of even getting anywhere near a record deal, so achieving that is the biggest highlight of our lives.' Now they had to prove themselves worthy of it.

CHAPTER SEVEN

THE CHAPEL

With the deal with Sony signed and sealed, the most pressing item on the band's agenda was to get in the studio and prove their worth as a major-label act. Right from the start, there was only one man they wanted behind the console: Colin Richardson, a legendary British producer with a list of credits that touched all corners of the metal map. He had first earned a name for himself at the more extreme end of the spectrum, bringing the aural terror of Liverpool's grindcore pioneers Carcass into focus, as well as producing for Napalm Death and Fear Factory. Two years previously he had even worked on *Casually Dressed & Deep in Conversation*, the debut of fellow Bridgend boys Funeral for a Friend. However, it was Richardson's work with Oakland's Machine Head – particularly the groove and guts of their 1994 debut *Burn My*

Eyes – that convinced Bullet that Colin was the man for the job. Matt even used to play the album as he got into bed, lulled to sleep by Robb Flynn's howls of anguish.

Colin dropped in on the band to hang out during a rehearsal session – an opportunity for both parties to get the measure of one another and assess whether the collaboration was going to work. Colin's reserved demeanour is completely at odds with the music he has made his name producing; he doesn't look like a metalhead, he doesn't sound like one and he doesn't indulge (at least, in public) in outrageous rock 'n' roll behaviour. Matt would later comment to Australia's *Beat* magazine that he seemed like the least metal person you could ever meet, saying, 'If you walked past him in the street, you'd have no idea he was Colin Richardson.' But he and the guys hit it off – within ten minutes and a few songs, Colin was on board.

And so, in the summer of 2004, the band headed to the studio to begin work on their first major release. The location was Chapel Studios. Set just outside the sleepy town of Alford in the Lincolnshire Wolds, the studio could pass for any other high-end rural idyll at a glance. And yet this converted Methodist Chapel and village school had played host to a diverse array of talent, not least Funeral for a Friend, Tuck's beloved Machine Head and Dub War – the predecessors of Newport's ragga-metal stalwarts Skindred. However, the sessions did not get off to the best start. They were driven to Lincolnshire by none other than Glyn Mills, the instrumental promoter in the Bridgend scene, and halfway up a hill it became clear all was not well with the transportation. 'It didn't break down to a stop, but the gearing... I couldn't get it into gear,' Mills says with a chuckle. 'We must have been half a mile or so at most from the studio, and it was struggling up the hill and they all had to jump out; we got to the top of the hill and they got back in, all the while slowly moving forward. I'll never forget that.' If the band had any delusions of grandeur now that they were a signed act, that experience would have surely brought them back down to earth with a bump.

The engineer on the sessions was Dan Turner, previously of Parkgate Studios, where Cradle of Filth had recorded much of their early 2000s output. 'There was definitely a buzz about [BFMV] around then,' Turner remembers. 'Colin and I were mixing another project at the time and he got given the offer to do it. He played me the demos, which I think were doing the rounds on the Internet somewhere. And immediately it was like, "yeah, this band are pretty cool."'

And it wasn't just on the Internet that the band were causing a stir – their short stints out on the road had also got tongues wagging. Turner said, 'I was also chatting the same day to my buddy Rob [Caggiano], who's the guitarist in Volbeat now, but he used to be in Anthrax. I mentioned that I was about to work on the Bullet EP and he was like, "wow – that band are amazing." It turns out they had just supported Anthrax. There was definitely a buzz about them, so I signed on, thinking this would be a great thing to do.' (This was the first time Bullet would get an endorsement from one of the Big Four of thrash – but not the last.)

The session was completed quickly – around two weeks of tracking and one week of mixing – with much of the material ready to go upon entering the studio. 'There was maybe the odd tiny little tweak here and there, but nothing really changed in terms of arrangements,' says Turner. 'Hand of Blood' was actually written in the studio and knocked out very quickly, as often the best things are. Another factor facilitating the speed of the recording was the band's solid preparation. 'For many bands' first records, they've rehearsed it to death. It was a really fast process doing the first EP because they knew the stuff off by heart, down pat.' Turner remembers being particularly impressed with Tuck's chops as a rhythm guitarist.

Naturally, a huge part of getting the right sound is getting the right gear and, as a fledgling act, Bullet were a little light on equipment. Turner recalled, 'As they were a young band without any money or serious endorsements, a lot of the stuff was hired. The drum kit and the bass was hired, though Matt had a really nice ESP, a Les Paul-type guitar. And we spent about two days trying to get the guitar sound; if I remember correctly, we ended up borrowing a producer called Andy Sneap's rig, which I think used to belong to [Carcass guitarist] Bill Steer.' Hearing the thunderous sound of a well-mixed set of drums and a time-tested amplifier from a metal veteran had an obvious effect on Bullet. 'The band were really excited to be doing it. When they heard the big drum sound for the first time, got the guitars going, there was definitely a sort of open-eyed awe about it all,' says Turner.

What Turner remembers most of the sessions is the ease with which everything came together, pointing out that often the process of making records is somewhat mundane. With that said, he was left with a sense of Matt's drive to succeed. 'It was their first record, and for the most part bands tend to be putty in your hand. But Matt was always a really focused and intense guy. Not in a difficult way, but in the sense that he knows what he wants, and he has an idea of how to go about getting it.'

Following completion of the EP, Bullet had just enough time for a five-date tour around the UK with 36 Crazyfists, this time playing London, Leeds, Glasgow, Edinburgh and Manchester. *Bullet for My Valentine* hit stores in the UK on 15 November 2004 and was put out through a licensing deal with Visible Noise, the same label that had released Lostprophets' debut *Thefakesoundofprogress* in 2000.

To properly understand the significance of the *Bullet for My Valentine* EP, it's important to understand the context in which it was released. Over in the US, 2004 had been a significant year for what would come to be known as the New Wave of American Heavy Metal, with Mastodon's *Leviathan*, Lamb of God's *Ashes of the Wake*, Killswitch Engage's *The End of Heartache* and Slipknot's *Vol. 3: (The Subliminal Verses)* all having been released by summer. But on UK shores, the metal revival was nowhere to be seen. Funeral for a Friend were still riding high off the back of *Casually Dressed & Deep in Conversation* and Lostprophets would top end-of-year lists with *Start Something* but both albums drew more from post-hardcore and American alternative rock than heavy metal. The mainstream's interest in guitar bands was swinging further towards indie, thanks to significant releases from Franz Ferdinand, Bloc Party and the ongoing Libertines saga. So, as an ominous swell breaks into the frantic opening riff of 'Hand of Blood', the message was loud and clear: British heavy metal was back.

As far as openers go, 'Hand of Blood' is a stormer. Even now, it puts everything that Bullet do best front and centre, from the furiously precise riffing and salvos of double-kick drumming through to a soaring middle eight of harmonised lead work. What's most striking is the ease with which the song moves between brutal, ballistic metal and melodic, vocal-led passages – a characteristic that would see the band filed away by much of the music press with the metalcore pack. But where the typical approach of the genre was to keep the screaming confined to a frenetic verse and open space in the chorus for some tuneful singing, 'Hand of Blood' demonstrates a deft ability to intertwine brutality and beauty throughout the song – a skill which the band pretty much encapsulate in their name.

'Cries in Vain' repeats the same trick but this time the song skips along on a galloping beat from Moose, accompanied by a riff that shows how naturally the band can express their melodic inclinations through their guitar work. Padge expounded the way in which the band develop their guitar parts in an interview with *Ultimate Guitar* and what's striking is how organic it seems: 'It usually all stems from one guitarist who will come up with the riff, but then we kind of work on the riffs, the harmonies, and take a look at it. We will all go into a room and then jam it out,' he explained. 'Me and Matt have actually been alongside each other for about ten years now, I think. So [...] when we go to do a harmony, we kind of know what harmony to do. We just interact with each other mentally.'

There's plenty of sophistication in the song structure too, with counter riffs and melodic callbacks creating a sense of irresistible momentum that carries through a two-part verse, a chorus, a middle eight and an instrumental coda. It's a neat piece of sleight of hand to have such complexity sounding so natural. Lyrically, Matt seems to be railing against a higher power that won't answer his prayers or offer him deliverance here. The band have remained somewhat tight-lipped about their religious beliefs throughout their career, although Matt did tell Eric Blair on his *Blairing Out Show*, 'I wouldn't say I'm a good Christian. I don't go to church or anything like that, but it is something I keep in the back of my head most days.'

Things change gear with the opening section of 'Curses' and the EP dips in intensity for the first time. The metal influences are backgrounded a little here, with the song following more of a post-hardcore or even nu-metal template. Lyrically, there's some respite from the tales of murder and mayhem, with Matt even indulging in a little tenacious optimism – 'when you feel like shit, you gotta keep on pushing'. With that said, the band still can't resist a brief but explosive passage of riffing as the curtain falls.

The band's love of Pantera creeps its way into the muscular

'No Control', a raging paean to anger complete with gang vocals and a pummelling palm-muted riff tailor-made for slam dancing. And as if composed specifically to sum up the EP in miniature, 'Just Another Star' seems to contain everything that has come before it in a single track – it opens with a scything, urgent riff a la 'Hand of Blood', moves into a grooving, muted section that recalls the one in 'No Control', has an unexpectedly melodic chorus and even throws in a couple of throat-rending death-metal screams for good measure. It's an eccentric and slightly schizophrenic burst of ideas that blasts past in just under three minutes but, as a demonstration of what the band were capable of, it's undeniably thrilling.

The release of the EP caused an immediate and somewhat unexpected stir. Matt would later recall that seeing the CD in stores was a defining moment for him but he wasn't oblivious to the fact that a real groundswell of support was building and that it was somewhat out of the ordinary for a band who had only released one EP. 'We just captured that nation's imagination at that time, and it snowballed across the planet. It was crazy,' he later said to Scuzz TV.

The excitement around the band was such that they sold out London's 1,000-capacity venue the Mean Fiddler (previously known as the Astoria 2) for their headline date on Valentine's Day 2004. The band had been there just four months previously as main support for 36 Crazyfists, and Moose recalls being terrified before the Valentine's Day show. Bullet hadn't released enough songs to fill the forty-five minutes required of a headliner, so they had to bulk out the set with new material. They opened with 'Her Voice Resides'. The audience, not having heard a note of it before, went crazy anyway. They followed with three more new songs that would ultimately find their way onto the debut, including 'Spit You Out' and '10 Years Today' and the fervour among the crowd was such that a frantic mosh pit broke out, with crowd surfers sailing over the barrier. By the time the band played 'Cries in Vain', the crowd's singing was so loud that they almost drowned Matt out. The sense of a band teetering on the edge of a huge breakthrough was unavoidable and Tuck dutifully noted that the show felt like 'a dream come true.'

It wasn't until May 2005 that '4 Words (To Choke Upon)' would be released, despite demos of the track having been available since 2004 (the demo features some slightly altered singing and guitar lines but is otherwise fairly true to the later studio version). But it must have felt sweet to finally get the song released, complete with an accompanying music video filmed at the Mean Fiddler show – the band had spent years in a dogfight of unsigned acts as Jeff Killed John and had their fair share of detractors to boot (Matt's former manager in his day job at the record store springs to mind). But the song is about as plain spoken a 'fuck you' to the naysayers as there could be; 'look at me now' goes the refrain, a joyous declaration of triumph to all those that told the band they should give up on their hopes of success. Musically, '4 Words (To Choke Upon)' is a maelstrom of squealing leads and furious drumming and, of course, comes complete with a huge, anthemic chorus. The video shows Bullet at their best, shot in a slick monochrome palette, with a throng of fans dutifully throwing the horns, crowd surfing and pressing to get closer to the band. It's a telling document of the intense support the band were eliciting in even these early stages of their career. The release would just about sneak into the Top Forty in the last position – though it did top the UK rock chart, beginning a streak that continued for their next six singles.

The feeling of a growing wave of excitement was amplified even further when *Metal Hammer* announced the nominees for its annual Golden Gods awards on 20 April, with Bullet singled out in the category of Best British Band – a full five months before their debut album would come to be released.

CHAPTER EIGHT

THE POISON

It was amidst this climate of anticipation – or, dare it be said, hype – that the band once again entered the studio with Colin Richardson to record their first album. However, Colin was not the only producer that the band saw as they were making *The Poison*. Both Padge and Jay have spoken of a trip to Canada to lay down some sessions with the producer Garth Richardson, often known as GGGarth, who has worked with an incredibly varied list of musicians – everyone from Mudvayne to The Melvins and, most notably, Rage Against the Machine. However, the sessions did not pan out, as Jay related in an interview with website *NZRock* in 2008. '[The label] said they'd pay for it and everything, so we went over and did like four songs or something, and we didn't have any input into the songs,' he claimed. 'He just took them, changed them all around, took all the parts out and made them sound completely different. We didn't even get a playback until he was finished, so we listened to the CD on the way to the airport. We were nearly in tears, it was horrible, it was absolutely horrible.' As such, the band were very happy to be in the studio with Colin.

According to engineer Dan Turner, roughly 90 per cent of the material was ready to go when they entered the studio, with the band writing songs throughout the latter half of 2004 and the beginning of 2005. Some material was written in the studio though, such as the composition initially called 'Helloween', in homage the Hamburg power metallers, which would later be retitled 'Suffocating Under Words of Sorrow (What Can I Do)'. After all, as Jay said to *NZRock*, '"Hand Of Blood" took ten minutes to write, and that was one of our biggest songs.'

Turner recalls that, in many respects, the sessions for *The Poison* felt like a continuation of the sessions for the EP. It had only been a few months and a quick tour cycle between the band finishing up on the latter. Most of the material was once again tracked at The Chapel, though Matt completed his vocals at Newport's Nott in Pill Studios, where the band had worked on their original demos. Considerably more time was spent on *The Poison* than the EP. '[Colin's] incredibly focused,' explains Turner. 'For want of a better word he can be very nitpicky. He has a real attention to detail, and he can't do with something that's not right, there's no sort of "that'll do". So he'll be there for hours sweating over the tuning of a snare drum or something – and he's absolutely right to do so, because in metal music, you can't get away with anything being even slightly untidy.'

This attention to detail didn't go unnoticed by the band either, who have commented numerous times on the respect they have for Richardson's approach. As Jay said to *NZRock*, '[Colin's] very particular, sonically... He won't rest until every single tom, every string, everything is sounding the best it can sound.' Moose was more succinct in his assessment, telling the blog *Rock Star Journalism*, 'He makes a metal record sound metal.' Jay also appreciated that Colin was not heavy handed in changing the arrangements for the songs, beyond suggesting the odd bass note, drum fill or harmony to round out the sound. Turner agrees that this style of production wins Colin a lot of fans among bands. 'One thing that bands really like about Colin is he doesn't try to get super involved in trying to change everything,' he says. 'He's not one of these guys that kind of says, "OK, let's cut the chorus in half, let's throw the middle eight over to this section, rework the lyrics here."'

One particular oddity that Turner notes from the sessions is the difference in guitar tone across the EP and *The Poison*. '*The Poison* and the EP are the exact same guitar set-up, and yet they sound completely different,' he explains. 'It's just a matter of where the mic's set up, the temperature of the air that day, and all kinds of different things. I was chatting to Matt a couple of years back, just having a drink and a catch up, and he told me – which I thought was really nice – that

61

ever since they recorded the *Hand of Blood* EP, they've been trying to capture that guitar sound again.'

Elusive guitar tones aside, all parties look back on the sessions and the resultant album very fondly. Colin Richardson would later say to *MusicRadar* online magazine, 'If I'm brutally honest, there are maybe only two mixes I've ever done that I'm even ninety-eight per cent happy with... I think that Chimaira's self-titled record, and maybe the first Bullet For My Valentine one, still stand up pretty well. But even then you hear it and you go, "Well, I still think the toms could sound better... Could the bass have been louder?"'

The album opens with 'Intro', a mournful instrumental composition that features additional string work by Apocalyptica, a Finnish trio of classically-trained cellists who had begun their career recording covers of Metallica before moving into original material. (Apocalyptica and Bullet shared a parent label, which sparked the collaboration.) 'Intro' serves as the first and only moment of calm on a record that barely lets up in intensity or technical accomplishment over its fifty-three minute runtime; it's a bruising, brutal listen that is, nonetheless, packed with huge hooks and infectious guitar lines.

'Her Voice Resides' is the closest the band come to classic thrash on the whole record, racing through a pulverising intro riff into exhilarating, throat-lacerating verses, all driven by the assault of Moose's drumming. Every riff and beat is tuned tight enough to snap and, though the chorus offers a brief let-up in the tension, it's only that – a temporary reprieve from the furious, unrelenting riffing. It all builds to a searing solo from Padge, a Kirk Hammet-esque, fret-melting performance that pops like a firework in the middle eight and burns away just as quickly.

Following 'Her Voice Resides' comes '4 Words (To Choke Upon)', which would also be added to the US version of the *Bullet for My Valentine* EP (repackaged as *Hand of Blood* and released on 22 August 2005 through Trustkill Records). But it's track three that offers the first real glimpse into Bullet's huge mass-market potential; a song that would propel them to superstardom and remain a fixture of setlists throughout their career to date. Titled 'Tears Don't Fall', it's a shift of tone from the frenzy of 'Her Voice Resides' and '4 Words'; an angsty, mid-tempo trip into a corrupted relationship with a chorus so big it practically has to squeeze itself out of the speakers. Like 'Her Voice Resides' – and much of the material on the album – the themes are of regret, emotional turmoil and failed relationships but it's hard to pin down the lyrics to a single clear interpretation. 'With bloodshot eyes, I watch you sleeping / The warmth beside me is slowly fading,' the narrator sings – is this the cold light of dawn after a one-night stand, followed by the backlash of a lover scorned? Is he trapped in a relationship with an individual who he cannot make happy, no matter how he tries? Or does the line 'the moment's died, I hear no screaming' point to an altogether darker reading; one of madness and murder? It's the simple ambiguity of the lyrics that makes the song such an effective tale of love gone bad and, no doubt, this had a huge part to play in its ultimate success.

The intro is lifted almost directly from the opening moments of 'Routine Unhappiness', a track from Jeff Killed John's 2003 self-titled EP that would prove to be particularly ripe for reinterpretation when it came to writing for *The Poison* (more on that later). '"Tears Don't Fall", that was an old riff that'd been hanging about for years [...] so we brought that riff out, added a few different riffs and organised it,' Jay told *NZRock*. The chorus is a big, melodic, half-speed singalong ready made for stadium shows but once again showing the band's knack for effortlessly kicking things up a notch within songs, the second chorus ushers in a furious double-time section, which steadily crescendos to another solo from Padge. Three successive songs and three lightning-fast, masterfully executed solos: make no mistake, there's no hesitation or coyness about technical ability here. Padge is staking his claim for guitar-god status.

It's Moose's superb command of his feet that drives 'Suffocating Under Words of Sorrow (What Can I Do)', with a double-kick drum rhythm propelling the verses as Jay and Matt trade hair-raising screams. Once again we're back in heartbreak territory but this time there's an undercurrent of tormented sexuality: the line 'she steps out from her under-wear, so beautiful' is delivered not in a seductive coo but in a despairing roar. The instrumental middle eight brings with it a harmonised duelling guitar line from Matt and Padge that's delivered over the recurring cantering rhythm, and the debt to Iron Maiden is obvious – though the tone of menace and emotional turbulence stops things ever becoming an exercise in imitation.

'Hit the Floor' was a late addition to the record, co-mixed by Colin Richardson and Andy Sneap at the eleventh hour (the same Sneap whose guitar rig the band had borrowed for recording). The main riff is a striking combination of Machine Head's groove, sped up and spliced with a classic Maiden-style lead line. Lyrically, we're still on the subject of corrupt romance but this time in far more fantastical territory; Tuck imagines himself as a stalker, pursuing his victim through dark streets. It's clear that there's an unhealthy obsession at the heart of the song but we're left unsure as to how things play out. 'I don't wanna hurt you,' the narrator insists, but is this an actual moment of clarity or the last protestation of a man who has already gone too far? It's a morbid subject matter, perhaps, but the positively euphoric middle eight takes the song on an unexpected left turn. This same middle eight can be heard in another version at around the three-minute mark of 'Routine Unhappiness' and the lyrics and vocal melody in the verses are pulled from another Jeff Killed John song, 'Eye Spy'.

'Eye Spy' was released in the early 2000s on a two-track EP and, despite the obvious crossover between it and 'Hit the Floor', it's amazing to listen to the two side by side. The former relies on brute force, with the guitar riffs so stodgy you could stand a spoon in them, and there is no discernible hook to be heard. There's still plenty of force in 'Hit the Floor' but it's a controlled power, with Matt's vocal trading with the guitar riffs, each unleashed in its proper place, and the rhythm section holding back on the fireworks until the song's climactic middle eight. In the five-year gap between the two songs being released, the band had evolved beyond all recognition.

'All These Things I Hate (Revolve Around Me)' is another old track featured on the Jeff Killed John demo of 2003, with the version here adding a considerable sheen and lustre to the production, as expected. The acoustic intro remains and the chorus is lyrically and melodically identical, though some additional lead work has been added and the drums have been noticeably stripped down in the verses. The biggest change comes in the middle eight. While in the original demo it's a fairly generic chord progression that sounds like it's been pulled from a Deftones B-side, by the time the song makes it to the album, the middle eight has turned into a far more distinct and memorable bouncing riff, at the perfect tempo to get a roomful of sweaty people pogoing. Clearly, over the two years since recording the demo, the band had learned a lot about the art of songwriting and they don't fail to wring every possibility from each moment. There's a marked shift in the timbre of Matt's voice over the two versions as well, more than can be attributed to the quality of the recording. While the pitch is the same, in the demo his performance has a thinner, more nasal quality, whereas the album version adds a significant amount of grit and gravel.

Tuck would later face criticism that some of his lyrics were too on-the-nose but there are times when a directness of approach can be incredibly effective. 'Room 409' is a perfect example. It's not the fastest, busiest or most technically challenging song on the record but the way in which the subject matter, vocals and repetitive trilling riffs come together makes it feel like one of the heaviest. For fans of metal with a harder edge, it's a clear highlight. 'I can't believe what I've seen, so scratch my eyes out / You, were at ease, on your knees, in his apartment' go the agonisingly blunt opening lines, so there can be no doubt what we're discussing: the shock and blind rage of catching your partner cheating. But there's something sardonic in the words too, the delivery of 'at ease' laden with black humour, just as the words 'now I can choose what to do with both of you' is laden with menace. You can't be much more plain spoken than to say 'I loved you / You hurt me' – but what else is there to say in such a situation? It's the lack of obfuscation in the lyrics that makes the song feel as heavy as it sounds. In terms of performance, Tuck and Jay are pulling out all of the stops too. There's a pleasingly unhinged quality to both voices as they move through screaming, shouting, singing, whispering and animalistic grunts in a convincing rendering of a man who's lost control. But for Matt, the song seems to say more about suffering the slings and arrows of life, rather than railing against them. 'Life is funny sometimes. It's never what it seems to be,' he told *SMNnews* shortly after the release of the album. 'A lot of [...] bands, their songs are about how good life is and how special love is. I like to say how it is. Like "Room 409", you catch a girl in bed with a dude, and that'll happen to a load of people. That's the way it is. Life isn't perfect.'

BULLET FOR MY VALENTINE

The slithering finger-tapped guitar line that opens 'The Poison' quickly gives way to a battering verse and the title track is impressive in its insistent pace, racing through a pulverising verse to a brief but insistently catchy chorus with barely enough time for the listener to catch their breath. There are plenty of highlights on display: the consummate ease with which Tuck switches between an insolent sneer and a furious roar in the verse is thrilling and Padge tears through the album's best solo at the track's midpoint, combining tapping that calls back to the intro with bluesy licks and even a touch of baroque-tinged arpeggio work. You can hear everyone from Eddie Van Halen to Stevie Ray Vaughn and Randy Rhoads in the brief few seconds of the blazing lead and it shows Padge to be an attentive student of rock and metal's greatest guitar players. By the time the song moves into its pneumatic middle eight – another moment clearly designed to get a room jumping in unison – it's clear that Bullet have winning over live crowds very much in the forefront of their minds.

'10 Years Today' is another highlight of the record and equally clear in its message, though it's altogether less fantastical and more sombre. The song is a tribute to a friend who died and, once again, it's the clear and unobscured nature of the telling that gives the lyrics their power. Rumours abound that the song is a tribute to a young man who took his own life and, though it's not entirely explicit within the song how the subject passed away, interpretations that it's about suicide are certainly feasible – 'How could you leave us that way?' sings Matt in the second verse, and later, 'I stood beside the wood that held you.' It's a powerful account of the guilt, helplessness and lack of closure that springs from a tragically young death and, musically, the song does an admirable job of representing sadness and anger alike; in particular, the desperation of the 'I'll bleed if you want me to' refrain. Incidentally, this line was again lifted from 'Routine Unhappiness', though the rhythm and melody has been altered.

Following 'Cries in Vain', the second track lifted from the self-titled EP, the album closes with the one-two punch of 'Spit You Out' and 'The End'. The former is a stampede of screamed call-and-response vocals leading into another big Bullet chorus, complete with neat harmonies and a rallying call to defy those that would bring you down. As raucous as it sounds, the song has a triumphant message of emancipation ('It's my life / I'm taking back what's mine / It's our time / to rise above'). Lyrically, at least, it's the most optimistic the album gets. The band even sneaks in a sample of a crowd cheering just before the final chorus – a kind of promise to the listener that the band would deliver on the live stage. Bullet would get plenty of opportunity to fulfil that promise over the coming years.

'The End' is not only the final song of *The Poison*, it also takes the ultimate end as its theme as Tuck laments the death of his lover ('your fingernails that marked my back now rot in earth,' goes the evocative second line). The tendency to gravitate towards extreme lyrical themes and imagery would become something of a modus operandi for Tuck, who preferred – particularly in the earlier stages of Bullet – to conjure up fictionalised stories as material for songs. 'Most of the songs are based around something that's happened, or I've seen or heard or know of, and as soon as I get to the second verse, I'm bored,' he told the *i heart guitar* blog in 2010. 'It's just not entertaining enough, so I'll take it off onto a more extreme level, use my imagination, and make the lyrics very visual.'

'The End' is an interesting blend of genres, with the more subdued verses having more than a touch of the Metallica ballad about them. But where the song moves to – a chorus of sorts, though the suspended chords make it feel more like a pre-chorus – is in the post-hardcore mould; a wrought and stuttering section that could have been featured on Poison the Well's *You Come Before You* (2003). The instrumental passage that begins at 3:27 is pure unfiltered metal, ideal for headbanging the graveyard soil from your hair, before returning to ballad territory as the music fades out. It's a fitting song to finish on, neatly summarising much of what we've heard before in one track; the themes of sex and death, the ability to switch between melody and brutality, and the seamless integration of genres.

The principal strength of *The Poison* is its depth. While the album inevitably has its stronger moments, there are no out-and-out weak links, nor is the tracklisting front loaded with quality while the tail end languishes with filler. This is a result of both the amount of time that the band had to build up to their debut as well as their notion that the album might be their last shot at making it after almost a decade of work. 'Our mentality was, when we were doing the EP and *The Poison*, that this could be our last shot,' Moose said in an interview with Scuzz TV. 'So we were trying to put the best songs forward.'

It's confident, brash and bold, with the metal and pop elements fused to the point that they feel inseparable. There's no sense of singles and album tracks, or songs for the metalheads and songs for the metalcore crowd. It's a complete vision of the way in which classic heavy-metal riffing could be incorporated into a modern and commercially savvy sound and it's an approach that Tuck says comes naturally to Bullet, with his love of Springsteen, Seger and Dylan teaching him to service the song first and foremost. 'The pop element to our music is totally a natural thing, it's what we've always done,' he said in an interview with BBC Wales in 2008. 'It's even what the name kind of represents. We always write the music first, then the lyrics and the melodies later. The music sets it up and whatever I feel like doing, whatever I think the song needs, I'll sing that. I don't care if it's pop or thrashy... I write what's best for the song.'

With recording complete for the album, the band headed out for the summer to begin touring in anticipation of the release of the record. They had no way of knowing that the tour would take the best part of two-and-a-half years.

CHAPTER NINE

ROAD DOGS

June was a particularly heavy month for the band's schedule, with festivals booked all over Europe, including Rock am Ring, Download and Graspop Metal Meeting. At the same time, they were fulfilling commitments on tour with fellow Welshmen, Funeral for a Friend. These shows proved to be particularly enjoyable for the band; they were on tour with their friends and the raucous crowd response made them feel as if they were playing headline shows. 'Every night it's been mad and they [FFAF] have actually told us please leave some people for us to entertain,' Matt told online mag *RoomThirteen*.

The Download festival was also set to be a huge moment for the band. It wasn't their debut, as they had played the Barfly stage shortly before getting signed. But this time they'd been bumped up to the Snickers Stage, the second-largest, which was beneath the main stage. As the undeniable Mecca of British heavy metal, a strong showing at Donington Park was a key chance to prove their worth as a solid live act in the run-up to the album's release. 'Andy Copin, who runs the show, is a big fan of ours, which helps us a lot,' Matt told *RoomThirteen*. 'He offered us a Main Stage slot this year but we turned it down to play high up on the Snickers Stage, and to be honest this was totally the right choice considering the fact we haven't even got an album out yet.'

The band played on Saturday, 11 June, fourth on the bill and sandwiched between Sweden's extreme prog pioneers Meshuggah and Virginia's Lamb of God, who were riding high off the success of their fourth album, *Ashes of the Wake*. The bill was topped by In Flames, a band Matt was heavily into at the time. It was a trial by fire but, by the time the band had worked through to the set closer 'No Control', they had the crowd in the palm of their hands; Matt demanded a pit and dutifully, one emerged. Bullet might have technically still been newbies but they looked for all the world like veterans.

While the band drew a lot of inspiration from metal icons that had dominated the 1970s and 1980s – Metallica, Maiden, Priest et al. – their fast-growing fan base was pulling in a lot of younger converts. Producer Andy Sneap (who had helped out on 'Hit the Floor' for the band's debut) saw them in 2005 and commented on his official website, 'The thing that struck me when I went to see [...] Bullet for My Valentine was how young the crowd was. Most of the kids going to these shows weren't even born when *Ride The Lightning* was out and Cronos and Thor were battling in the pages of *Kerrang!* So I guess we are seeing things come full cycle again with the influences of the past twenty years thrown in.' Tuck, too, was not oblivious to the resurgent popularity of metal and how his own band was being carried along in the wave. Speaking to *SMNnews* on the health of the metal scene, he said, 'I think it's good, a lot healthier than it was five years ago. It's back to being rock and metal again, which is a good thing for metal bands. The audience we attract, it's a new generation of kids and it's their first taste of metal. They're all fourteen to eighteen, and it's a very influential time for them.'

However, the youth of Bullet for My Valentine's audience was also a cause for mockery and derision by some sections of the press, who saw the band as a kind of entry-level metal band. *Stylus Magazine* wrote in its review of *The Poison* that 'their sole intention is to make soundtracks for fifteen-year-olds to throw themselves violently at other fifteen-year-olds in provincial towns up and down the country,' and that 'nobody who has started shaving will be able to sit through an entire hour's worth of these guys.' Still, snobbery about the youth's tastes is nothing new, even though they've consistently proven themselves to be influential tastemakers in music. (And, in fairness to *Stylus*, they did note, 'No Welshmen has gotten the pit moving with that sort of crushing ferocity since Aberfan.')

Bullet weren't the only band in 2005 that was capturing attention and winning fans with a fresh take on classic metal, taking the well-worn conventions of the genre and placing them in a fresh context. 2005 was also the year of two major releases that would coincide with *The Poison* and create the sense of a new movement, where the experimental and punk-inflected edge of post-hardcore and metalcore had previously stood dominant. The first of these, released in March, was Trivium's *Ascendancy*. The second studio album of the Florida quartet was released on legendary imprint Roadrunner Records and met with a significant amount of critical acclaim for its razor-sharp take on classic thrash fused with post-hardcore influences. *Ascendancy* would go on to win the Album of the Year Award from *Kerrang!* magazine.

Come June, Huntington Beach outfit Avenged Sevenfold released *City of Evil* and, while they were already well established on the metalcore scene, the record saw them incorporate significantly more influences from their native California – most notably, Guns N' Roses, as well as the guitar gymnastics of Van Halen and just a dash of Motley Crue's sense of theatre. Singer M. Shadows had all but abandoned his screaming voice in favour of a characterful tenor and the overall effect was to make the album sound like a hard-rock record from the late 1970s that had been speeded up and shot with adrenaline. Both albums sold well across Europe and in America, with Avenged's single 'Bat Country' in particular pushing them to the forefront of the rock scene more so than ever before. The overall effect was undeniable: classic influences were coming back and Bullet had timed their move into the public eye perfectly.

June also saw Bullet play a three-song set at the Astoria for the *Metal Hammer* Golden Gods Awards, where they had been nominated in the category of Best British Band. They lost out to Lostprophets who, according to one report, were the target of loud booing. Thrash pioneers and former tour mates Anthrax took home the Best Metal Band award and also closed the night with a half-hour set. Bullet would have more success at the Kerrang! Awards the following month, taking home the gong for Best British Newcomer, and it was here that Matt also had the pleasure of meeting his idol Robb Flynn for the first time. 'He was so important to me growing up, and he was such a nice guy, really chilled out,' Matt told *Kerrang!* 'He instantly knew who we were and he was well into it. A real gentleman.'

Following the triumphant Download appearance and the *Kerrang!* win, there could be no doubt that Bullet were on an upward trajectory but, behind the scenes, things were not completely without complication. The band had already been gigging, writing or recording solidly for the best part of a year with very few days off in between and, with the recording sessions being slotted in around a heavy touring schedule, the first signs of strain were beginning to show. As Matt told *Guitar World*, the lack of rest manifested itself as a panic attack: 'It started as pins and needles in my left arm, so I just sat down and picked up a guitar,' he said. 'I tried to get my fingers moving, but I couldn't play. Then the sensation went straight down my leg and thighs, and to my face. I guess it was kind of a wake-up call that I needed to chill out a bit.' With a week of rest, Matt was back on the horse.

'Suffocating Under Words of Sorrow (What Can I Do)' was released as a single on 19 September, with the black-and-white palette of the '4 Words (To Choke Upon)' video carried through to a moody promo shot by filmmaker Miha Knific. The atmospheric clip sees the band playing in an eerily lit cave, interspersed with shots of ballerinas tumbling and twirling and strobing shots of the band in close-up. There's more than a hint of the 1948 movie *The Red Shoes* about it, with its themes of madness and the pressure of love. Filmed on location in Slovenia, the band ventured three miles down into the pitch black to film. Padge told the *FasterLouder* website it was one of the 'most metal' places he'd been to. The video was getting heavy rotation on the digital channels that supported the rock and metal markets in the UK and, upon release, the single cracked the UK Top Forty chart – a first for Bullet – entering at number thirty-seven. The infiltration of the mainstream had begun.

The Poison got its official UK release on 3 October 2005 and immediate responses were mixed. The album won plenty of plaudits for its furious duelling guitar work, technical proficiency and melodic sensibility; *Drowned in Sound* awarded the album nine out of ten, calling it a 'horribly, unashamedly metal affair' that showcases 'the enviable ability to seamlessly blend raging power with wonderfully crafted songs.' Others were not so convinced; while *AllMusic.com* praised it as a 'well-produced, solid effort', they felt that the band would need to work hard to gain a foothold in the US, saying, 'Seeing as they're now trying to take over American hearts, it would be nice to see future attempts to distinguish themselves more from the new-school pack.' And so began the notoriously fractious relationship between the band and the media. There would be no shortage of magazine-cover shoots and lead features awaiting them but the criticism would grow vociferous too – almost in direct correlation to the band's growing fan base.

But whatever the reviewers had to say, the success of the album was undeniable. Seventeen days after its release the band were headlining the Astoria in London – a marked jump from their set at the Mean Fiddler just months prior. And despite the capacity being almost double, they had once again sold it out. Support came from fellow Bridgend outfit Hondo Maclean, as well as Arizona's Scary Kids Scaring Kids and Candiria – a Brooklyn band getting plenty of attention, combining metalcore with more eclectic influences. The band played a fourteen-song set drawn from the EP and the album, marching on stage to the pre-recorded 'Intro' before tearing into 'Her Voice Resides'. This time the band had the advantage of playing to a crowd who had got a chance to get familiar with their material – granted it was only two-and-a-half weeks but the audience had clearly been doing its homework. The fervour that was on display at the Mean Fiddler had not been diluted by the increased size of the crowd and, by the time the final sombre strains of 'The End' were drawing the set to a close, it was clear that Bullet for My Valentine had the material and the presence of a fully-fledged headline act.

But, as much as the UK had been longing for great twenty-first-century heavy-metal act, the band had designs on other markets – mainly, the poisoned chalice of the US. British groups had long coveted America as the ultimate indicator of 'making it'. But such is the size and diffuse nature of the country, bands can – and have – wasted years of their career doggedly touring around the States only to return to Europe with their tail between their legs. In fact, the entire concept of breaking America had become something of an albatross around the neck of British acts; The Jam had famously failed to convert any of their huge success in the UK to stateside sales and, since then, many of the UK's bright young things fizzled out as soon as they took the trip across the pond. The failure of Britpop to drum up even a fraction of the excitement it had done in its native country had put paid to any idea that Britain was the arbiter of good taste in music. Robbie Williams, perhaps most notably, had signed a record-breaking £80 million contract with EMI and, despite becoming one of the most successful recording artists in history, could not translate his huge sales to America. Success in the USA cannot be bought, even with major-label cash.

And it wasn't just rock, indie and pop's young upstarts that had failed to match the globe-conquering stature of their forebears. Britain is generally agreed to have the best claim as the home of heavy metal and it certainly forged a reputation as a world leader in the late 1970s, when the so-called New Wave of British Heavy Metal swept the globe with Iron Maiden, Saxon, Motörhead and Judas Priest at the fore.

But since then, most of the huge strides in the development of the genre came from elsewhere, with the USA having almost sole claim to the birth of thrash metal and grunge, and Scandinavia taking the lead in the extreme-metal stakes (albeit with the notable influence of Napalm Death and Carcass, of Birmingham and Liverpool, respectively). The upshot is this: British heavy metal was due for a new star.

Not that Bullet would have necessarily had such lofty ambitions when they set out on their first US tour in the November of 2005 with It Dies Today. They were more concerned about being loyal to their roots. 'A lot of the bands go over there and try to take on the American lifestyle, you know, start speaking like an American and acting like one,' Jay said in an interview with *Ultimate Guitar*. 'We're British and we just want to go over there and show them what we can do.' A deal had been inked with Trustkill Records, who had already released *Hand of Blood* and were prepping to release *The Poison*, and It Dies Today were a fellow Trustkill act – many notable post-hardcore and metalcore bands had been on the Trustkill roster, including Eighteen Visions, Hopesfall and Poison the Well.

However, this was not the US run on which Bullet would conquer the land of the free: a drunken night in Phoenix ultimately derailed the tour. While the details are (understandably) somewhat hazy – Matt would later tell an interviewer that it was the time when he was the most drunk he had ever been in his life and that he has no recollection of the night at all – the story goes that he and Jay got into a friendly playfight, which, no doubt fuelled by booze and the enthusiasm of being on tour in America, got a little out of hand. In the fracas, Matt ended up smashing his ribs against the bunk area of the tour bus and, upon waking, was so badly hurt that he was struggling to even draw breath. One trip to the hospital later and the guys realised that there was no way Matt could continue with the tour. 'I'd bruised all my ribs and it was terrible. The boys were really worried 'cos they'd never seen me like that before,' he told *Popworld*. (Matt would later recall how, a month after the initial injury, a lump appeared where he had struck his side and, on tour in Germany, his girlfriend accidentally pressed against it, causing it to move from his ribs down to his back.)

After a few days off to recover from Matt's injury, 2005 ended in European tours with Apocalyptica and then with Chimaira and Dark Tranquillity, who were alternating the headline slot. But it was during the run with Apocalyptica that the first signs of an issue that would almost bring Bullet's story to a premature end began to show itself. On 2, 3 and 4 December, Bullet had to cancel their shows again owing to a 'severe throat infection' and Matt was ordered to rest his voice. It was little more than a brief break in the schedule but it marked the first troubling signs of what would develop into a much larger threat to the band's existence.

The momentum that they had built up through 2005 was carried through into 2006 with the release of the official video for 'All These Things I Hate (Revolve Around Me)'. While the band had starred in a couple of stylish clips before, this promo took things to a new level, with a markedly American setting and a loose narrative about a girl experiencing premonitions of her boyfriend's death. Directed by Scott Winig, it's an effective accompaniment to the song in as far as it doesn't nakedly translate the lyrics into a story and there is a suitably ominous payoff in the closing moments as it is revealed the band is playing in front of a coffin (presumably of the boyfriend in question).

Life on the road also continued apace in the first months of 2006, first in the UK as part of the KXXV tour, celebrating the twenty-fifth anniversary of iconic British rock-and-metal magazine *Kerrang!* They were out on the road with Still Remains, Hawthorne Heights and Aiden. The latter, a Misfits-indebted group from Washington playing a kind of horror pop punk, had been enjoying their time in the sun thanks to the release of *Nightmare Anatomy* at the end of 2005.

The tour culminated in a sold-out show at Brixton Academy, which was filmed and ultimately released as a standalone DVD. It offers a snapshot of the incendiary performances that Bullet put on in these early days, well before budgets and the scale of venues allowed for the arena-scale production that would later become part of the show. The first thing that's evident on looking back at the DVD now is the age of the fans clamouring to get close to the stage as the camera sweeps along the barrier, their faces a picture of unrestrained anticipation. This truly was a youth phenomenon, with a whole new generation experiencing metal for, most likely, the first time. It must be strange for the band to think of themselves being the first gig for many early teens, just as Moose and Jay got their first taste of live music from Metallica.

From the moment Matt steps on stage (clad in an Aiden shirt, no less), he is the consummate frontman. Before he's even played a note, he is standing with his legs spread wide, one hand aloft, absorbing the energy of the crowd. In 'Her Voice Resides' he steps to one side and casts his head back during the chorus to indicate that it is their turn to sign and they readily do so. Indeed, there's more than a touch of James Hetfield about the figure that Tuck cuts on stage, his mic positioned slightly lower than his mouth so that he has to set up in front of it with his legs bent; it has the effect of making him appear like a sportsman, braced and ready to take the brunt of whatever force he's about to come up against. Perhaps it's a trick he learned from seeing Metallica, or perhaps it's one he learned from the rugby field.

Beyond simple showmanship there's a real strain of musicianship on show too, clearly honed from the previous year's intense touring schedule. Matt and Padge execute every lick and riff with clinical control, including the solos, where not a note is dropped. Moose's muscular, no-nonsense drumming is flawless and Jay proves to be an unexpected ace in the hole of Bullet's live show, his screams in support of Matt's lead vocals all the more hair-raising live than on record.

For 'All These Things I Hate (Revolve Around Me)', Matt climbs a ramp to an elevated platform behind Moose's kit and demands to the crowd, 'If you have lighters or mobile phones, put them up in the fucking air right now.' The message is clear; this is metal in all its pomp and ceremony, disregarding the anti-rockstar approach of the 1990s and embracing the frontman's role as ringmaster of a particularly noisy circus. 'All These Things I Hate' was due for release the following week and its video had been receiving heavy airplay from MTV2, Kerrang! TV and Scuzz, the digital channels largely owning the rock-video market in the UK. The crowd sing the intro along with Tuck, with enough passion to convince that the song was going to do well. Sure enough, it would enter the UK Top Forty at twenty-nine – the band's highest charting single to date.

A particular treat comes towards the end of 'Spit You Out': on the recorded version that appears on *The Poison*, the band had practically foretold their own future with a clip of a crowd roaring as Tuck introduces the band played over the skeletal bass and drum breakdown. And here it is, enacted in the real world at a sell-out show at Brixton Academy, with 5,000 rabid fans clapping on command. The biggest crowd response is probably saved for the suitably boisterous 'No Control', where more than one circle pit can be seen swirling in the old theatre's standing section, but it's 'The End' that closes the set, with Jay's almost death metal-esque howls giving the song's heavier sections a particularly nasty edge.

On reflection, the band have stated that they'd rather not even know that a DVD was being filmed, such is the extra pressure it puts on the performance, but there's no hint of nerves on display here. It might have been a long road for the band to get to Brixton but those nine years of slogging away without recognition or reward, paying to play shows while working mundane day jobs, had paid off. The band don't look like a new act with barely an album under their belt; they look as if they were born on stage. In 2006 Padge was asked where he'd like to see the band by 2010 and he replied, 'By then I'd love to be doing arena tours... full-on rock, pyrotechnics, ramps, you name it. I want to be putting on the biggest show we can put on, as well as being the biggest band in the world, if you know what I mean.' Judging the band on the promise of *The Poison* DVD, they don't look that far from it.

The Poison would see its US release on Valentine's Day 2006, with the album sent out to press packaged in a red heart-shaped box, and the album immediately struck a chord with American fans. In the first week the band shifted 10,000 units, which got them to 128 on the Billboard 200, but number 1 on the Heatseekers chart (Heatseekers tracks the week's top-selling albums by new or developing acts, defined as those who have never appeared in the top 100 of the Billboard 200). Sales continued to tick along nicely, with 8,000 sold each week for the fortnight after release week. They may not have been setting the charts on fire but, as Tuck pointed out at the time, the band was yet to release any singles from the album in the States. And regardless, big sales had never been on the band's mind when they made the album. As Padge told

Ultimate Guitar, 'We didn't make the record just to sell. We just kind of wrote the songs for ourselves.'

After the release of the record, the band embarked on a major tour around the US in support of Rob Zombie. Zombie – real name Robert Cummings – rose to prominence in the early 1990s as the founding member of White Zombie, a New York art band that offered an alternative to the Seattle sound, saturating the airwaves with a heady mix of horror imagery and industrial-tinged heavy metal. Since 1998 Rob Zombie had been pursuing a solo career, further distilling the hard industrial edge and B-movie influences. In the early part of the new millennium he moved into film, directing the horror films *House of 100 Corpses* and *The Devil's Rejects* but by 2006 he had moved back into music, releasing *Educated Horses*, his third album as a solo artist. His guitarist on the tour was John 5, best known as the former guitar player in Marilyn Manson's band.

Bullet for My Valentine had previously been scheduled to tour with Finnish melodic death metallers Children of Bodom. But with their profile on the rise Stateside, they were asked to join the Zombie tour. It was a no-brainer: the venues were three to four times the size those that they would be playing on the Bodom run, so the decision was made to switch (Through the Eyes of the Dead would replace Bullet).

Beginning on 16 March and due to run all the way through to May across some thirty-four dates, the tour was a great opportunity to get some serious US mileage under their belts at mid-sized venues while on the road with a genuine veteran. Eight or nine days in, Matt spoke to *SMNnews* and appeared to be having a relatively good time; the shows were going well and, while he stated that there was 'no bonding' between the band and the Zombie crew, he did point out that they were 'very quiet guys who keep to themselves and do their thing,' describing the situation as 'very polite'. Even Lacuna Coil, the other band out on the tour, were singing Bullet's praises and noting the great responses all the bands were enjoying from the crowds.

But even at this early stage, some signs of discord were apparent. When asked by *SMNnews* if the band had had any chance to toy with big production, Matt replied, 'No, this tour is very limited, we're not allowed to do shit on this tour. We're basically told what to do, when to play, and shut up the rest of the time.' It didn't take a detective to realise that something was not quite sitting right.

On 6 April it became abundantly clear that all was not well on the tour. On the official Bullet for My Valentine message board, a couple of users had been griping, seemingly about the cost of T-shirts and songs that the band had not been playing during their set. Tuck, who had been known to post under the user name 'Mattie', replied on the thread personally with the following message:

Yo, check it. We get just 30 minutes on this Zombie tour, that's it!!! So there's not a lot of time to fuck around. Apologies for not playing all these, but shit, man, you can't please all the people all the time. Next time, bro.

As for the merchandise, Zombie makes us price match him so, yup, it's fuckin' $40 for a T-shirt, which is insane, I know. Greedy money-grabbing fucks. We're only allowed two pieces of merch, too, which sucks ass. Unfortunately, being first on a tour like this sucks, but it's gotta be done. As I write this, I'm sitting on the fuckin' floor of the venue 'coz we don't have a dressing room again, 'coz fuckin' Zombie takes them all for him, his band and crew. Basically, we are shit to him, but fuck it – if this is what it takes to get a name over here, then it's gotta be done. I'm not one to fuck around with words, so yes, we are not being treated well on this tour. Oh yeah, we don't get a soundcheck either. Fuckin' pissed at this tour, man.

Later that day, the message had been picked up and reported by *Blabbermouth.net*, a major site for rock-and-metal news, and the furore was immediate. Many were supportive of Tuck for exposing the practices that support bands will sometimes have to fall in line with when on large tours; others said that the invective showed a lack of humility. Andrea Ferro of Lacuna Coil – members of which had previously expressed their support for Bullet – felt that it showed a lack of experience on Matt's part, rather than a genuine bad attitude. 'When you open and you are the first out of three bands, many of the venues can't hold the dressing room for everybody, so it's normal that you sometimes have to sacrifice a little bit,' he said in an interview with *HeavyMetalSource.com*. 'Probably they got some different kind of success in the UK in the beginning and they think that they paid their dues, but I believe that they still have to pay their dues, like everybody [...] But I think they're really nice guys, they're a very good band. It's just a matter of unexperience [sic], I believe.'

In any case, Matt was quick to issue a full and frank apology, posting once again to the official Bullet for My Valentine website's message board. Noting that he was both hungover and trying to deal with personal issues back in the UK while on his first real tour of the States, he commented, 'We really have been totally fuckin' thrilled to have the chance to play on this tour and are grateful for every new fan we make. It means everything to us to be able to play our shit for new fans. I'm really sorry to have offended anyone and look forward to putting this behind and getting back to the metal.' However, the damage was done and, two days after the initial message was posted, Bullet were off the Zombie tour.

Over the coming months the band would comment many times on the debacle and it's fair to say that they felt they had reason to be disgruntled. In an interview with *InTheNews.co.uk*, Moose claimed that the band were emailed a list of 'stupid rules' prior to beginning the tour, one of which was that the tour was dry. 'I mean, coming from Wales, touring, we like to have a drink,' he pointed out. And while reiterating that he wished he hadn't said anything on the situation, Matt did later say to Sirius Satellite Radio's *Hard Attack* that he wasn't happy with the way the band were treated. 'We did seventeen shows in total with him before we left the tour, and that doesn't include days off and stuff in between, and not once did he say a "Hello" to me, the guys, our crew, anybody. That was total fucking disrespect.'

The whole Rob Zombie incident turned out to be something of a storm in a teacup. Not only did it afford the band the chance to take some time off – three weeks, in fact, which they spent writing their next record – but all the column inches it inspired may have had a positive impact on album sales. Not for nothing does the saying exist: there's no such thing as bad press. However, Moose has since stated that the band regrets being so outspoken in their early days, remarking that, while they stand by everything that they say, they have since learned that it's wiser to keep their opinions between band and crew.

Besides, the time back home would no doubt have been enjoyed by the band. They might have been an international touring act by this point but one source was keen to relate that at no point has the band's success affected them as individuals. 'To be fair, when the boys come back home they're just lads out for a quiet drink – or a loud one,' says Glyn Mills, the Bridgend promoter who had hosted Jeff Killed John many times in Bridgend and beyond. 'I remember once I was walking home. My brother had just passed away, and they saw me from the pub; they dragged me in and I didn't put my hand in my pocket all night, the lads looked after me. That's the way they were, and that's the way they are, there's nothing pretentious about them [...] They've kept close to their friends too, and I think they're still very level headed.'

The band had other commitments to fulfil, not least repaying favours that had been paid to them as they were on the rise. In April Apocalyptica's second Best Of collection was announced, entitled *Amplified // A Decade of Reinventing the Cello*, for which Matt had contributed guest vocals to a previously unreleased track called 'Repressed'. The track also features Max Cavalera of Sepultura and Soulfly fame, although the pair of frontmen did not share a studio to lay down the vocals. 'Finding good timing for it was really a project... they both were on tour so it was not possible to get them to same studio,' explained Apocalyptica member Eicca – Cavalera recorded his parts in Munich, while Matt took time off from the Dutch leg of the Bullet tour for his. The track itself begins with a taut, hypnotic riff, with the distorted cellos taking on a mechanistic, industrial quality. Parts of the verse almost sound like they wouldn't be out of place on a Swans record, with the pre-chorus a particularly atmospheric passage. It's almost a shame when the more conventional chorus comes in, with its big sung hook. With that said, it's an interesting and highly enjoyable collaboration and more than fair compensation for the work that Apocalyptica did on *The Poison*'s 'Intro'.

Just as the Zombie tour was ending, Bullet also announced their first ever headline tour in America, running throughout May. As Matt rightly pointed out, it was a chance to show American audiences what Bullet were really made of, in a full headline set. Packaged as the Trustkill Takeover, support came from two other bands on the Trustkill roster. First up was Roses are Red – an alternative rock/emo outfit

– and main support came from Walls of Jericho, a highly promising metalcore band from Detroit that drew on classic thrash and heavy-metal acts much like Bullet and were fronted by a flame-haired, powerhouse of a frontwoman named Candace Kucsulain.

At the same time as Bullet were on the road with their own promising support acts, they were also being booked to support bigger and bigger acts themselves. The first of a trio of legendary rock bands who Bullet were pulled in to play with was Guns N' Roses, who were in the midst of the marathon recording-and-release process for their sixth album, *Chinese Democracy*. Depending on what yardstick you measure by, the record had already been in development for over a decade and hopes were high that it would finally see the light of day at some point in 2006 (as it happens, *Chinese Democracy* would not be released until late 2008). Regardless, Guns N' Roses – now sans Slash, Duff McKagan and Matt Sorum, as well as Izzy Stradlin, who had left in 1991 – announced the Chinese Democracy Tour 2001, a continuation of a tour that had technically begun in 2000. Bullet were booked to support on their four warm-up shows at the Hammerstein Ballroom, as well as on a number of European dates.

Anticipation leading up to the gigs was at fever pitch, not least because Axl's time-keeping had been the subject of some derision on recent tours. Queues for the shows were reportedly stretching five blocks and there were enough celebrities packed into the VIP area to suggest the suburbs of Los Angeles were half-empty.

Playing beneath bands the size of Guns N' Roses was a new experience for the band, not just in terms of the scale of venues but also in the reaction of the crowds. It's often the case – if not exactly customary – that fans of classic rock acts give the support act a hard time. While acknowledging to the *Talking Metal* podcast that the experience was 'amazing', they were also forced to admit that the opening night was packed with 'hardcore Guns fans', saying, 'some people were being pretty mean, but we expect that.' With that said, the Hammerstein shows were widely considered a success for Guns N' Roses, with the setlist light on experimentation and packed with the hits people had paid to see.

Axl's behaviour, however, was less impressive to Bullet, particularly on the later European dates, with Tuck saying to Denver's *Westword*, 'How would you fucking feel if you were standing on an arena floor for fucking six hours waiting for your idol to come on, and then he plays half an hour and fucks off?' (He did add that Bullet themselves were treated very well.) Matt would later comment to *Revolver* magazine that what he saw during this period served as a 'prime example of how not to fucking act on tour.' There was also a sad coda to the stint when Bullet were forced to cancel two dates in Finland and one in Norway owing to the ill health of Jay's father.

A typically busy summer-festival period marked the middle of the year, with the band once again heading to Download, this time third from the top on Sunday's Main Stage billing. In two short years the band had graduated from being an unsigned band on the Barfly Stage to the Snickers Stage to a Main Stage act and a huge draw. Only Funeral for a Friend and Guns N' Roses were placed higher. But the real treat for the band came in August when they got the chance to play the second of the three huge support slots that would come to define their year. But for the band, it had to be the most significant. It was the band that had first inspired Matt to pick up a guitar, the songs that Bullet would first play together as a group and the first band that Moose and Jay had ever seen live: Metallica.

Earlier in the year Bullet had contributed to a special edition of *Kerrang!* released in tribute to the twentieth anniversary of *Master of Puppets* – Metallica's third studio album and first bona fide masterpiece (it was also the last to feature bassist Cliff Burton, prior to his untimely death in a 1986 bus crash). The edition came with a CD entitled *Remastered*, which featured each track of the album covered by a different artist – Tuck's beloved Machine Head took 'Battery', Trivium handled the title track, Mastodon contributed a cover of the funereal instrumental 'Orion' and Funeral for a Friend brought proceedings to a close with 'Damage, Inc.'. It was down to Bullet to handle the album's midpoint highlight 'Welcome Home (Sanitarium)', a track famously inspired by the Kesey novel *One Flew Over the Cuckoo's Nest* and widely considered to be among the greatest songs that Metallica ever wrote. No pressure then. But the track was the band's first choice when presented with the project. 'When we were asked we didn't need any time to think about it, we said yes immediately,' revealed Moose in an interview with *Metal Rage* ezine. 'We were lucky enough to choose the song we wanted to play, [and] we chose "Sanitarium".'

Whatever responsibility Bullet may have felt to do the track justice, they do an admirable job navigating its complex landscape. While Tuck can't quite match Hetfield's snarl, the higher tone of his voice – along with the added vocal harmonies – casts the song's internal narrative in a new light, suggesting innocence defiled where the original suggests the weariness of age (although, interestingly, Hetfield was actually younger at the time he recorded the original). The song's melodic guitar breaks are pulled off with all the grace of the original and, come the song's double-time middle eight, the band let rip with the dual screaming they used to great effect on *The Poison*, hammering home the message of anger and frustration finally let loose. It doesn't quite match up to the power of the predecessor but criticising a band for being less Metallica than Metallica would be ludicrous.

At any rate, the cover proved one hell of an icebreaker between Bullet and Metallica and they were relieved to discover that the old maxim 'never meet your heroes' did not prove true in Metallica's case. At the first date the band were due to play – at the GelreDome, Holland, on 6 August – drummer Lars Ulrich knocked on Bullet's dressing-room door unannounced to introduce himself. 'Him [Lars] and the rest of the band and the crew made us so welcome,' recalled Tuck in a 2008 interview with *Westword*. 'Anything they could do for us, they would, and they'd hang out in our dressing room, talk as friends. It was a totally bizarre, surreal experience, but at the same time it showed us that was definitely the route we want to go in the future.' Indeed, the combination of their prior disappointing experience as a support act and the joy of discovering that Metallica were every bit the gentlemen they had hoped they would be had a profound impact on the band. They continued to hold them as a model for behaviour on tour, preferring to personally choose their supports if possible and ensure that other acts felt welcome to hang out in the dressing room to jam, drink and relax with them.

Though getting one-on-one time with the heroes of their youth must have felt like a childhood fantasy fulfilled, perhaps even their wildest dreams wouldn't have allowed for them performing on stage with the band. Bullet, Trivium and Avenged Sevenfold were all invited on stage to sing backing vocals for 'Die, Die My Darling', the Misfits cover featured on *Garage Inc.* Even the most cynical old-school metalhead couldn't deny the sense of a torch being passed. The triumvirate of Bullet, Trivium and Avenged Sevenfold were at the vanguard of a metal revival, each with their distinct flavour and influences, taking cues from the past while presenting a thoroughly modern offering. Trivium were the obvious Metallica enthusiasts, with their primal and unrestrained blend of thrash and metalcore set off by Matt Heafy's throaty vocal, Avenged Sevenfold had the swagger and melodramatic bent of Guns N' Roses and Bullet's nimble duelling guitar work has the distinct melodic thrust of Iron Maiden. During this summer – and particularly during the

Metallica support dates – the three bands would spend a considerable amount of time together, with Matt noting that all three bands had similar ambitions and goals and yet were able to co-exist without rivalry getting in the way. 'It seems like it's kind of meant to be, like it's part of a cycle,' Matt observed to *Revolver* magazine. 'It just seems right, in a spooky way.'

It wasn't the last time Bullet would share a stage with Metallica – in Estonia they appeared as main support and, shortly after stepping off stage, Bullet got a knock on the door of their dressing room. This time it was Metallica's tour manager, passing on the message that Metallica would like them to come up on stage to sing backing vocals to 'So What?', a cover of the obscene classic by the Anti-Nowhere League that also appeared in *Garage Inc.* (key lyrics: 'I've fucked a sheep / And I've fucked a goat / I rammed my cock right down its throat'). There were around 105,000 people in the audience. To this day it stands as the largest crowd that Bullet have ever appeared in front of and they did so to sing the words 'so what, you boring little cunt.' 'To jam with them on stage and get to know them and get drunk – it's something that doesn't even register and it's so untouchable, it just doesn't compute in my brain,' Matt would later tell *The Aquarian*.

In the same month as the Estonia gig with Metallica, Bullet poured oil on the flame of their building reputation with the release of 'Tears Don't Fall', one of the undisputed highlights of *The Poison*, as well as one of its most radio-friendly moments. The accompanying music video still stands as a high watermark for the band. Shot in crisp but cold hues of blue and grey, the performance segment of the video sees the band indulging in that most melodramatic of rock 'n' roll tropes – an impromptu performance in the pouring rain. But it's the promo's narrative element that caught the most attention. It concerns a young couple, clearly with a taste for living life on the wild side, on a road trip through some dusky backwater of the States. They check into a motel to have suitably wild motel sex but, by the next day, the male protagonist has clearly had enough of the girl's advances as he shrugs off her touch in their run-down pickup. He has to stop to refill the gas and she once again tries to kiss him. This time he forcibly pushes her away, which she, in turn, responds to by dancing seductively in the spilled gasoline before he abandons her at the side of the road. One thing is clear: this relationship is volatile and something's probably going to blow before the end. Except, it doesn't. In a neat little twist, our troubled heroine catches up with her former lover in (yet another) seedy motel, where he's locking lips with another girl. She douses the pair in petrol from a jerry can but, as she drops her Zippo to the floor, we realise it was not petrol at all but water. She blows him a kiss and walks away, dignity restored and the upper hand gained.

If you want to make a man sexy, give him a Flying V guitar and stick him in a rainstorm. Tuck had been the focus of a fair amount of admiring glances prior to this point but this is probably the moment that propelled him from rather handsome guy in a metal band to full-on alternative sex symbol (just check out 'Bullet for My Valentine fan fiction' on Google if you're in any doubt). The way in which the video neatly circumvented the standard needy-girlfriend-goes-crazy paradigm to portray the female lead as troubled but ultimately in control probably did much to win the hearts of female fans too.

The video was shot, at least in part, in Miami, where the band were playing the Global Gathering in Bicentennial Park. It's actually the second version of the video – an alternative exists with the same performance shots but an entirely different plotline, concerning a girl who wreaks revenge on her lover with the help of a witch doctor – this version was included with *The Poison: Live at Brixton* DVD. At any rate, the version that ultimately made it to networks is far superior and undoubtedly contributed to the song's success and, while the song did not chart as high as 'All These Things I Hate (Revolve Around Me)' in either the UK or the US, it has arguably outstripped it in terms of staying power. The only (admittedly minor) controversy the band would have to address was the omission of the screaming section in the pre-chorus. Where in the album version, Matt lets rip with his trademark guttural howl, for the radio version, Matt sings the lines. It's a sad fact that bands will sometimes have to bow to radio pressure to get their songs played – particularly in America, where the influence of radio networks over sales is significantly higher than in Europe. 'It's just TV, radio politics, such bullshit,' Matt explained in an interview with Rock Am

Ring Offstage, where the band had delivered a blistering set. 'You've just got to play the game. It's not something that we agree with or approve of.'

One version of the single also came packaged with a cover of Pantera's 'Domination', lifted from the album *Cowboys From Hell*. The lead vocal on the track is a remarkable performance, quite unlike anything else Bullet has ever recorded, and, with Moose showing off his double bass chops throughout the track, it makes for a considerably more frantic experience than the original. The band were steadily building up quite a back catalogue of cover versions; in addition to 'Welcome Home (Sanitarium)' and 'Domination', the band had also contributed a cover of Ozzy Osbourne's 'Crazy Train' for the *Kerrang!* magazine's 25th Anniversary Special Edition, released earlier in the year (the album also featured buddies Avenged Sevenfold covering Pantera's 'Walk', and a cover of Dio's 'Holy Diver' by Killswitch Engage, which would end up being a breakout hit for the band). Bullet's contribution sticks pretty close to the template laid out by the original, with a few harmonic embellishments here and there. The range of Matt's voice is a natural fit with Ozzy's, even if it doesn't quite have its distinctive strained quality.

The band also took time in the summer to attend the ceremonies for both the *Metal Hammer* Golden Gods and the Kerrang! Awards. *Metal Hammer* had nominated them in three categories – Best UK Band, Best Live Band and Album of the Year – and they also performed a live set before ultimately taking home the award for Best UK Band. At the Kerrang!

Awards, Bullet were also honoured with the Best Single gong for 'Tears Don't Fall' and they were clearly happy about it. A wonderful video exists, reportedly taken after the event, that shows members of the band laying drunken waste to a back room that appears to have been set up for photo shoots. They are accompanied by a few other usual suspects, including Bring Me the Horizon's singer Oli Sykes. Just as a woman manages to usher most of the marauding partygoers out, Moose gets hold of a fire extinguisher and starts gleefully spraying everyone in the vicinity. Padge sums it up to the camera like so: 'What the fuck do you think this is, the Brit Awards or what?'

If, indeed, Bullet did most closely resemble Iron Maiden out of the new-school trio of themselves, Avenged and Trivium, it's only right that the band should have rounded out their impeccable new touring CV by sharing some dates with the British metal icons. And sure enough, in 2006 the call came that Iron Maiden would be embarking on a US tour throughout October in support of their new album, *A Matter of Life and Death*, and Bullet had been requested as the opening act. They had not just held their nerve during the Guns N' Roses and Metallica dates, they had positively excelled, proving that the savage riffs first penned in sweaty rehearsal rooms in Bridgend could fill stadiums around the world.

But preceding Iron Maiden would be a new challenge. Maiden fans could be notoriously unkind. In his 2001 stand-up/spoken-word show, *Up For It*, Henry Rollins – the hard-headed, quick-witted, muscle-bound punk icon who spent five years as the frontman of legendary hardcore band Black Flag – described supporting them like this: 'If you are in front of eighteen to twenty thousand Iron Maiden fans, the upside is, they only want to see one band. The downside is, you're not in that band. You are the irritant. They hate your guts.' He goes on to vividly describe the chanting, booing, cursing and general torrent of abuse that could be expected. 'I've been there, I've done it, I've survived it,' he offers. 'My back still hurts.'

Not that Bullet were ever about to turn the gig down. They'd been making some serious inroads across the US all summer as part of the Warped Tour (itself notorious for the gruelling nature of the schedule) and, as a result, their profile was continuing to grow. Come August, *The Poison* had shifted an impressive 75,000 units and it had already been heavily hinted to them after completion of the Metallica dates that an Iron Maiden support slot could be on the cards. The band considered Maiden the final piece of the puzzle to round off a year of dream bookings. And, for their part, Maiden were delighted to have Bullet on the bill too, having been impressed by their work ethic. 'Bullet for My Valentine will be with us on most of the dates in the USA and they're a band that's been out on most of the major festivals this year and apparently have been picking up plenty of awards,' said bassist Steve Harris to *Metal Forever.com*. 'They've been working really hard but in my book that's the best and only way to become a great band.'

But sometimes, no matter how hard you're willing to

work, how finely tuned your live set is, or how much grit and heart you put into the performance, you're still going to come out slightly worse for wear. So it transpired for Bullet. Moose commented that he found it frustrating that the fans wouldn't even give the band a fighting chance and, on many occasions, they were chanting for Maiden before Bullet had even played a note. As he pointed out, Bullet were and remain huge Maiden fans themselves and were no doubt just as eager to watch the band's set as the fans taunting them. But even an exciting new British metal band that would regularly pay tribute at the temple of Maiden could not appease the crowds. 'I wish the crowds could have been a bit nicer to us,' Moose said to *Dose.ca*. 'It's not very nice when you're trying to do a set and, all through it, fifteen thousand Maiden fans are chanting for Maiden to come on. You've got to laugh. You can't be upset for a long time.' One attendee at the Agganis Arena show in Boston was the blogger from *Observes From the Satellite*, whose disdainful analysis sums up what one imagines was the attitude of a lot of the crowd: 'If they [Bullet for My Valentine] thought they were going to gain any extra fans or sell any extra records by opening for one of the world's most distinctive and exciting heavy metal bands, they were totally mistaken – and if [Iron Maiden co-manager] Rod Smallwood thought that adding them to the bill would pull in more of the younger crowd, he's totally mental.'

But the band didn't have too long to lick their wounds. Straight off the back of the Maiden gigs they were back in Europe for a headline tour, with all of November booked up with UK dates. They brought two new pals over from the States with them to support – Orange County's Bleeding Through and San Diego's As I Lay Dying. It was to be a triumphant homecoming – the victory lap at the end of a hugely successful year where the band had taken their debut album global, wrestling the giant of America and coming out on top. The tour was set to end at the 5,000-capacity Hammersmith Apollo, in London, bookending the year with the same triumphant air that it began – the show at the Brixton Academy.

But the extreme demands of the year's touring schedule had not come without their consequences and, by the time the band made it to Edinburgh on 20 November – just six dates into the tour – the set had to be cut short due to Matt's 'fading lungs'. Initially, hopes were high that some of the tour could be salvaged but, as more and more dates were rescheduled, it became clear that this was more than a mere rasp in the throat. Matt's condition worsened and ultimately developed into a full-blown bout of laryngitis. A US run the band had booked for December, with the likes of Hawthorne Heights, Sugarcult and Sparta in support, was hastily scrapped. The world rumbled on; would-be concert goers were disappointed but it was just another cancellation among cancellations – an inevitable chapter in any touring band's story. Except it wasn't. Fans had no way of knowing it but Tuck was battling with a condition that would threaten to end his and the band's career.

CHAPTER TEN

THE LONE STAR STATE

ooking back on the release and touring cycle for *The Poison*, Matt is able to see what an exceptional circumstance it was. 'When I think of that album, it was the most exciting time in our lives,' he told website *Artist Direct*. 'We've become a lot bigger and more successful since that album, but I don't think anything will ever beat the feeling of when that album came out and did what it did for us in the sense of success and being pushed to the top of the tree. It was crazy. It brings back bad memories too because I was pushed to the point of crazy physical and mental fatigue. It was an absolute whirlwind of good and bad memories – most good though [...] They were very special moments.'

However, right in the midst of the whirlwind, there was no time for reflection and every spare moment had to be dedicated to maintaining the momentum that the band had built up. The forced time off while Matt was on vocal rest was put to good use, as the band spent three weeks writing songs for their sophomore effort, before fulfilling the UK dates in January that they had been forced to cancel in December. They were not oblivious to the pressure that was on the band; second album syndrome is a well-worn concept in music but the chance of falling prey is only amplified with huge breakout success. There was, without doubt, a buzz around them as Bullet entered the studio to record their debut but the expectation surrounding the second album was a whole different ball game. As Moose commented to *FaceCulture* in 2014, 'We had all our lives to write those songs [on *The Poison*]. And then obviously, once you write that and you become so big, and you've got six months to write another one, that's when the pressure's on.' But this was not to be a directionless effort; the band knew where they wanted to go with the new LP. 'We want to be more metal all across the board,' Matt reported to *Revolver*. 'On their second album, a lot of bands try to please their record company by doing something more commercial. We didn't want to fall into that trap.'

Writing for the new record had begun almost the day after *The Poison* was released and had continued throughout the year, pulled together from snatches written in soundcheck, in hotels or at the back of the bus, as so many second records are. Soundchecks are an important ritual for the band, as Jay's bass tech, Calvin Roffey, explained to *Performing Musician*: 'The band always come in and soundcheck, and they'll normally play four or five songs, just because they enjoy playing,' he said. 'They don't really need to, because everything's the same. They've got the same monitor guy, the same desk, the backline's the same, and they rarely change anything in their monitors. But they come in and play, mainly just because they enjoy it.'

Typically, a riff would emerge from Matt or Padge and it would catch someone's ear and get recorded on a phone, just to ensure it wasn't forgotten. Then, whenever the band had a chance, they'd jam it out, filling in gaps and stitching different riffs together. Come September 2006, they had built up a fair bank of material and headed to The Dairy Studios in Brixton with Colin to begin demoing material. But during the demoing period, a new song came along that completely changed the direction of the new material – it was the song that would ultimately become 'Scream Aim Fire'. In light of the song's relentless, driving riff, the other songs they had written no longer seemed up to scratch. As Jay said to *NZRock*, 'We had like seven or eight songs ready to go, already written, and then one day we sat down together and "Scream Aim Fire" came up, it was just like "wow, look at this riff we've put together." We finished the song in literally ten minutes and that just changed the whole direction of the album.' The material that had been prepared was scrapped and the band endeavoured to meet the standard set by 'Scream Aim Fire' (and, with this story in mind, it's easy to see why the album was ultimately named after the song). The next six songs came together in just a week and the band had the foundation of a new record – although there was some suggestion that not everyone was as taken with the faster, harder new sound. 'I think the label maybe wanted us to just mellow it out a bit more in parts so we could get more radio play, but we put our foot [down] as we always wanted to make a metal record anyway,' Matt told the website *Planet Loud*. 'Maybe we've been kind of limited in the past and we're now better with our instruments, so I think we just wanted to put out what came naturally.'

There was no question as to who the band wanted to produce – they had been delighted with Colin Richardson's work on *The Poison* and Richardson himself was keen to work on the follow-up too. Recording the sessions with Richardson was Matt Hyde, a London-based producer and mix engineer whose extensive CV includes names like Machine Head, Slipknot and Trivium. Hyde had first met Richardson while working in-house at Miloco, a Bermondsey studio where Richardson was working with Funeral for a Friend – the band had been booked in to rework the song 'Juno' from their 2002 *Between Order and Model* EP. After working on the track that would ultimately become 'Juneau' – and the band's breakout single – Colin asked if Hyde would like to work with him on all of *Casually Dressed & Deep in Conversation*, Funeral for a Friend's debut album, and their working relationship began. The professional chemistry between the two was immediate, with the skills of one the perfect complement to the other. 'We got on very well personally, really well,' says Hyde. 'It was just a good combination; I learnt so much from him about recording techniques, especially for the production of heavier music, and he also had someone who was completely up to date with the modern methods using Pro Tools, beat detectiving, splicing drums onto a grid, and so on. We just kind of seemed to work well together in the studio environment.' Hyde also worked on some of *The Poison*, travelling up to Andy Sneap's studio in Belper to track 'Hit the Floor', so a relationship with the band had already been forged.

With the team in place, the only outstanding question was where the album would be recorded. Members of the Bullet team were keen for it to be taken to America, with two studios in the running, the first being The Plant in San Francisco Bay – formerly The Record Plant – where Metallica had recorded much of their 1990s output. The second was Sonic Ranch, in Texas. Hyde said, 'While Colin and I were doing the first Fightstar album [*Grand Unification*], a conversation came up with the band and management about going out there, because at the time the exchange rate was 2.2 dollars to the pound or something. We were using a studio called Townhouse and the band realised how much money was being spent on studio time. They went to the management and said, "Why don't we go to America and do it? Even if you factor in the flight costs we're going to be spending half the amount we are." So that seeded the studio into the management's head and when it came time to do the Bullet record, it was management who suggested it.'

Ultimately, it was decided that the isolated location of Sonic

Ranch – the nearest town, El Paso, is around half an hour away – would make for a better working environment and the band packed their bags for a stint in the Lone-Star State.

Sonic Ranch is a truly remarkable place. Reckoned to be the largest residential recording studio in the world, it's a sprawling complex situated within 2,300 acres of pecan orchards, which is the prime source of income for the area. It comprises no less than five studios, as well as five houses for accommodating bands and crew, one of which is a seventy-year-old, twelve-bedroom hacienda complete with pool, den and workout room. Make no mistake: it is the fantasy playground of every muso's imagination, which, of course, means that it is also home to a head-spinning amount of beautiful gear, from the vintage and esoteric to the modern. 'The studio is a hobby for the owner, who is a very interesting guy,' says Hyde. 'He just so happens to have an incredible collection of studio equipment and guitars. He flies off to guitar shows and events and buys lots of special-edition guitars. The studio itself was all based around a beautiful old Neve desk – it was huge – and the collection of outboard gear was just phenomenal.'

Some of that gear found its way onto the record, with one guitar in particular standing out to Hyde – a Gibson Les Paul constructed to mark the hundredth anniversary of the guitar maker. 'When the company was started, they put aside some of the wood that they made their first factory guitars from,' says Hyde. 'On their one hundredth anniversary, they did a run of one hundred guitars made from this wood. And [studio owner] Tony had one of them.' The guitars came with a very special feature – a genuine diamond inlayed into the headstock to form the dot of the 'i' in Gibson, and the guitar even came with its own certificate of authentication from a jeweller. Unsurprisingly, the guitar was kept in the studio owner's private collection but this was no status symbol kept under lock and key – many of the clean guitar sounds on the record were tracked using the guitar.

Back during the recording of *The Poison*, the band had a limited budget and no endorsements from the major musical-equipment suppliers, so equipment had to be hired in. But those days were behind the band and, this time around, they had as many gear variations to try as they pleased. 'The amount of equipment we had, I'd never known anything like it,' recalls Hyde. 'Just starting with the drums – Moose has got the Pearl endorsement, and they sent us so many drums. I think we had twenty odd snares to try out – in the end we used a Chad Smith signature snare. And the number of cymbals stuck in my head; we had one hundred-and-thirty cymbals to try, all the ones Zildjian had sent us, and all the ones that were in the studio as well.' There was even a full-time drum tech on hand to take care of tuning and head changes – 'a real Texan dude, always talking about hunting and guns.'

In terms of amps, the band opted to stick with the rigs they had been touring with for the past year. They had two amp heads each – Matt was playing Peavey 6505s and Padge Mesa Boogies – but with the band having done so much touring in the States over 2006, they also had both European and American rigs (this is standard practice for international bands who want to save on the costs and risks of shipping). So the band had their European amps shipped over too, to give them a grand total of four identical models each of the same amp to try. But when it comes to equipment, what appears identical might sound anything but, especially in the forensic environment of a high-end recording studio. 'We had four 6505s, and the UK ones sounded noticeably better than the American ones,' says Hyde. 'We had to use a transformer because they were 240 volts. The American ones just sounded a little bit flatter and more lifeless than the European ones. But Eddie Van Halen always used to play European model amps. He said it was basic science; 240 volts is gonna sound better than 110 through tubes.'

The band had arrived in Texas with eight songs ready to go and, during the seven weeks that they spent in Texas, a further four or five were written. Musically, the band were clearly happy with how smoothly things were going. They had been drawing a lot of influence from the 1980s, absorbing the guitar gymnastics from bands of the era, as well as soundtracks to classic movies. The upshot was that the band was incorporating a lot more solos and leadwork for Padge than in previous efforts. Matt offered an update on the recording to *Guitar World* prior to his vocals being tracked, saying, 'We're really excited about the new stuff, which is a lot more technical, guitar-wise. It's heavier and more uptempo, and there's a lot of eighties guitar work, but it sounds really modern. If I can get the vocals to sound as good as the music, it's going to be a great album.' Another big switch in mentality for the band was the use of major keys, which the band had entirely stayed away from in the past – major keys have the effect of making songs sound happy, upbeat or hopeful. Matt had some reservations when he began using major keys, fearing that the approach would be deemed poppier and that accusations of selling out or bowing to corporate pressure would be levelled at the band as a result. But the quality of the songs ended up being the arbiter. As he put it to *Westword*, 'I was like, "Fuck it. This is a great sounding song." [...] I'm not the sort of person to be afraid of trying something different.' The band were gunning for a more varied sound; the strength of *The Poison* had been in the volume of songs that they had to choose from when it came time to hit the studio but now they were aiming to push every facet of their sound to the extreme.

Matt was, in fact, tracking a lot of the guitars himself, which is not unusual for metal bands, as Hyde explains: 'He [Tuck] does all the rhythm and most of the overdubs and things, and Padge plays the solos. It's quite a common thing when you're tracking an album, especially for metal bands which is all built around riffs: for the tightness you often have one guitarist do both the left and right guitars. That way you have the same technique, the same feel in the way that they down pick. Although you can have two guitarists that individually have good timing and good technique, if you put them together it often won't sit perfectly and give that power that you want.' Hyde recalls being impressed with Matt's chops as a guitar player. 'I would say he had very good technique. He's really solid. None of Bullet's riffs are that complicated, but that's one of their best strengths – he doesn't over complicate things.'

While the music was being laid down with no great impediments, vocal tracking was proving much more complex. Matt's voice had not fully recovered from the laryngitis that had forced cancellations at the tail end of 2006 and it meant that the band were all but prevented from laying down the vocal parts. The vocals that would ultimately appear on the album were not actually recorded in Texas at all but finished months later back in Wales with Martyn Ford and Jeff Rose, who had helped out on the Bullet demos (doubtless an environment Matt felt comfortable in). But looking back, Matt remembers that Colin's calm and patience was of huge importance during the sessions in Texas. 'Even when things were bad with my voice and we were in the studio for three weeks without one word being put down on Pro Tools, there was no negativity,' he said to *Revolver*. 'He never got frustrated. He was just like, "No worries – we'll take a break for a few weeks and come back." He pretty much kept it together when times were getting really ugly.' The initial idea was to get tracking finished in Texas but, when it became clear that it wasn't going to happen, the time that had been booked to mix the album back in London had to be cancelled. Without a delivery day, the album became 'stuck in limbo', as Hyde puts it.

Despite the anxieties surrounding Matt's voice, the band found plenty of time to cut loose and have a little fun, Texan-style, while at Sonic Ranch. Matt bought a quad bike and Padge bought a scrambler, which they used to tear around the pecan orchards. Matt later donated his quad to the owner upon leaving for future guests to enjoy. Being a dyed-in-the-wool Texan, the owner also had an impressive gun collection, which he would allow the band to shoot around the ranch. Suitable precautions were taken, of course, though Hyde does recall that, at one point, Jay was throwing cans of Coke in the air as Padge attempted to blast them with a shotgun, like a cowboy's take on clay-pigeon shooting. Moose was presumably banned from handling firearms after his dalliance with the fire extinguisher at the Kerrang! Awards. 'They were comfortable, especially Jay,' remembers Hyde. 'Jay was so enthusiastic and a bundle of fun the whole time. He really embraced it, the whole Texan thing; went out with the studio owner and bought himself a hat and a pair of cowboy boots.' Moose later commented that he found the whole experience far less stressful than the recording of *The Poison*, despite the extra pressure that the success of that record had placed on them.

CHAPTER ELEVEN

A LUMP IN
THE THROAT

With the music for their second record in the can but the vocals conspicuous in their absence, the band headed out on the road in the States again, touring throughout April and into May with Escape the Fate and Confession. Come summer, they returned to the UK. It was once again awards season, with the band nominated for Best UK Band at the *Metal Hammer* Golden Gods, held at Camden's KOKO; they took home the award but *The Sun* reported that the band were the subject of booing, just as Lostprophets reportedly were in 2005. While it's probably overstated to call this the start of a backlash, it's interesting to note a major British tabloid taking such an interest in the band. It has often been noted that the UK, unlike America, has a troubled relationship with ambition and success and, accordingly, the

British press is notorious for building up and then tearing down public figures. Regardless of the accuracy of the story, it was clear that the band's success had not gone unnoticed by the mainstream press. The night was positive for Machine Head, though, who were riding high after a triumphant set at Download a few days prior. In addition to appearing live, Robb Flynn took home the prestigious Golden God gong.

Recorded output was kept up over the summer with the Deluxe reissue of *The Poison*, which added four extra tracks to the original thirteen on offer. As well as the cover of 'Welcome Home (Sanitarium)', the album included 'Seven Days', a mid-paced track with a motorik verse propelled by a simple, catchy riff and a big pop-rock chorus that would sit quite comfortably on radio. The song plays a nice trick of interspersing melodic sections into the plainly aggressive verse, with the repeated yell of 'Fuck it!' like a battle cry. The rapid shifts from anthemic passages into pounding, repetitive riffing gives the song a kind of schizophrenic quality. There's little doubt as to the violent subject matter of 'My Fist Your Mouth Her Scars', another original track included on the Deluxe Edition but, as with much of Bullet's output, the exact details of the story are not clear. It appears to be a fantasy of revenge against an individual who has hurt a woman dear to the narrator and the fury is powerfully communicated through the matched rhythm of the guitars and the vocals in the verse. There's also a particularly effective pre-chorus that borrows from melodic death metal, with Moose delivering a crushing blast beat under shrill screamed vocals doubled by a fast-picked guitar line. It's a neat example of Bullet's skill in incorporating the subtle variations that define metal sub-genres in one track. Both 'Seven Days' and 'My Fist Your Mouth Her Scars' were originally released as B-sides for 'All These Things I Hate (Revolve Around Me)'. They appear on the reissue of *The Poison*, alongside the 'Welcome Home (Sanitarium)' cover and an acoustic version of 'Tears Don't Fall', which proves that Bullet's instinct for huge, catchy melodies remains intact when songs are stripped back to just a guitar and vocals.

The band also contributed another Metallica track for *Kerrang!* magazine, this time for a compilation entitled *Higher Voltage!: Another Brief History of Rock*, released in June 2007. This time it was the classic 'Creeping Death', which the band used to cover in their days as Jeff Killed John, and the practice had clearly paid off. The version more or less sticks to the script, adding very little in the way of embellishments and none of the original's power is lost in the translation. Of particular note is Matt's voice in the version. It has more than a touch of the young James Hetfield about it, considerably more so than in their previous Metallica cover, and it's small wonder considering the vocal trouble Tuck was experiencing around this time. 'We chose this song as we pretty much knew all the parts as we used to play it years ago before we got signed,' Tuck relayed to *Kerrang!* 'We only spent about eight hours on it from setting up to mix so we're so happy how it came out. It's pretty fucking heavy! I'm sure Lars [Ulrich] and the boys will check it out, they loved our "Welcome Home (Sanitarium)"

121

cover from last year's *Kerrang! Remastered* album so maybe we'll get to jam it with them on the upcoming summer tour!'

However, the dream of jamming 'Creeping Death' with Metallica that summer was not to be. They were set to fulfil a number of dates in the summer, including Metallica support slots – one of which was a dream gig at Wembley Stadium. However, the obstacle of Matt's recurrent vocal issues proved insurmountable and it was decided that Matt would be admitted for an emergency tonsillectomy, a procedure whereby the tonsils are removed from the pharynx. Bullet pulled out of the dates. The fact that Tuck's heroes Machine Head replaced them would have provided little comfort.

A tonsillectomy is a common treatment for recurrent bouts of tonsillitis and laryngitis but changes in the timbre or range of the voice is a possible side effect of the surgery. This would be a concern for an average patient but, for Tuck, it was a huge risk. He had already cancelled a huge show in an iconic venue with the band he most idolised in his formative years. Alongside the rest of Bullet for My Valentine, he had spent a decade or more working to get where he was, with the last eighteen months a near non-stop marathon of touring and road life; the follow-up to *The Poison* was undoubtedly going to be a huge make-or-break moment for the band; the point at which all of their hard work would come to fruition or the moment in which the bubble would burst. It's hard to imagine the amount of pressure that was riding on the success of the operation and the amount of trepidation Matt and everyone associated with him must have felt as he prepared for the surgery.

Matt's first thoughts upon waking from the procedure were not good. Rather than coming round with a renewed sense of hope, he opened his eyes to discover that his uvula had swollen so badly that it was blocking his windpipe and he was having difficulty breathing. In his panic, he managed to find the emergency call button and hit it; doctors rushed in and were concerned enough to discuss the removal of the uvula altogether, which would have markedly increased the risk of significant changes to his voice. Fortunately, his airway was cleared and recovery could begin but the road would be long and the emotional fallout severe.

The tonsillectomy was no quick fix. As the band got back to the studio – this time with producers Martyn Ford and Jeff Rose, partly in the reassuring surrounds of Newport's Nott in Pill studios – Matt found that his voice simply was not performing the way that it used to. The technique he had developed since birth to control his voice suddenly didn't apply anymore. Even speech was difficult, so the prospect of delivering vocals for a highly anticipated record must have been terrifying. Some tracks had to be recorded line-by-line, or even word-by-word, as Matt couldn't get through a whole section in one take. His confidence was shot and he was having to relearn how to use his voice as he went along. Speaking with the then titled *myYearbook* website, Moose would liken it to 'trying to run with one leg.' Lyrics were also proving to be a sticking point; the band's process had always been to write all of the music and then add vocal parts as the final stage in the creative process but the mental strain of not being able to sing in the way that he used to had manifested itself as a bad case of writer's block too.

The low point of the whole episode came when the band were leaving rehearsal after another frustrating session. Matt and Moose were parked next to one another and, as they were getting into their cars, Matt opened his mouth to bid his bandmate farewell but no sound came out. He had lost the ability to project his voice even a few metres in casual conversation. It would be psychologically harmful for anyone but for someone whose livelihood and identity was irrevocably tied to their voice, it was nothing short of devastating. 'I didn't feel like I was me anymore,' Matt told Scuzz TV. 'I didn't really know what had happened, who I was; I was skin and bone. It was fucked up, man.'

Of course, the burden was also carried by the rest of the band. Jay noted how, from the time of the release of the first EP, the band had barely stopped touring; their ascent had been nothing short of stratospheric, with venues steadily increasing in size, achievement following achievement, accolade piled on accolade. In tandem with the success had come ever more demanding schedules, so the band didn't have time to stop and reflect on what they'd achieved or how far they'd come. They were too focused on the next show, the next session, the next step. But once Matt was admitted to hospital, the band were forced to stop and forced to take stock of the last few years. It suddenly dawned on them: the scale of what they'd achieved, the places that they'd seen, how far they'd taken the songs that they wrote in their bedrooms as young men. Suddenly, their position seemed precarious. Continued success was not a guarantee. There was a very real chance that it was all going to come to an end.

There were even some talks at this time about getting another singer in to replace Matt, with Matt continuing as a guitarist only. It's not clear how far these discussions got – possible names have never emerged in the press – but the band did not want to continue without Matt. 'None of us wanted that and the label didn't want that,' Jay said to *NZRock*. 'So we all helped him through it. I physically made him stay in his house. I went round to his house and made him get his guitar out and sing the songs he was having trouble with, over and over again until he was pissed off. I would not give up on him, man.'

Finally, with patience and perseverance, the band were able to wrap up sessions for their second album around November of 2007. Finishing in itself felt like a huge achievement to Tuck but, in retrospect, he has stated that the decision to delay recording while the vocal issues were addressed was a mistake. 'The only thing I regret in our careers is not finishing that record and sitting on it for six months,' Matt explained to Scuzz TV. 'It wouldn't really have affected anything, and the vocals on that record... I can't even listen to it anymore. It doesn't even sound like me, because I was just doing anything to get the sound out of my throat.'

CHAPTER TWELVE

SCREAM AIM FIRE

The first glimpse of the follow-up to *The Poison* arrived as an early Christmas present for fans, on 13 December 2007. But if any of them were expecting a dose of Christmas cheer, they were going to be disappointed. The track, titled 'Scream Aim Fire', was a blistering indictment of the horror and injustice of war and it came with an accompanying music video that had the song's themes writ large. It's no surprise that the band chose it to be the first promotional release for the record, given that it was a hugely significant track in defining the direction for the album, and it immediately ignited excitement for the new release.

The song opens with a salvo of drumming that immediately brings to mind artillery, before the introduction of a rapid, palm-muted, tremolo picked riff. Thrash is the most immediate reference point, with the song foregrounding many of Bullet's classic influences while playing down the elements of their sound that had previously seen them pigeonholed as metalcore. The screamed vocals are restricted to the breakdown, with Tuck instead adopting a grizzled, snarling tone. Most of the vocals that you hear on the final version are in fact demo vocals lifted from the band's initial sessions at The Dairy, prior to Matt's tonsillectomy, and there's certainly no weakness in the vocal performance audible to the casual listener.

Where *The Poison* was typified by big melodic choruses that contrasted with a fast-and-furious verse, 'Scream Aim Fire' refuses to let up throughout the whole track, with a sense of unstoppable momentum carrying right through to the huge, off-kilter breakdown that leads into Padge's brief but explosive solo. As far as hooks go, here Bullet prove that you don't need melody to make something irresistibly catchy; the song's repeated refrain of 'over the top, over the top' is every bit as memorable as it is dramatic, thrilling and terrifying.

Lyrically, the track represents new territory for the band too. Heavy metal has a long history of addressing the subject of war – Metallica did it with 'Disposable Heroes' and, most memorably, with 'One'; Sabbath had 'War Pigs'; Judas Priest tackled the topic head on with the plainly titled 'War'; and Iron Maiden took inspiration from historical conflicts with 'The Trooper', 'Run to the Hills', and '2 Minutes to Midnight'. In short, a song about war is a must for any self-respecting heavy-metal band. The only variation is how you tackle it.

Tuck's approach manages to be wide reaching and personal at the same time. Rather than adopt some sort of moralising general position on war as a whole, Tuck instead puts himself in the position of a soldier in the heart of battle and, rather than speaking about a specific conflict, he relates the experience of one individual. The result is incredibly effective. Coupled with the relentless riffing and driving rhythms, the song is terrifying and exhilarating at the same time and is an effective critique of violence in war without having to explicitly say so, or compromising the unabashed thrill of the song itself. Particularly interesting is the line 'God has spoken through his conscience'; it's a surprisingly thoughtful line about the presence of God – or, at least, some kind of innate moral code – within every person, even in the most wicked circumstance, where men are brought together for the express purpose of killing one another. Matt and Padge worked on the song in the studio together and have successfully added a valuable perspective to the canon of war songs.

The video is a straightforward affair, showing the band playing in a warehouse in front of white drapes that hang from the ceiling. Projected on to the drapes are scenes of warfare from various periods. The concept was originally more complex, involving an actual crowd and scenes shot with night-vision cameras, though, for whatever reason, the version that finally made it to air was a considerably more streamlined edit. It might have had something to do with My Chemical Romance's video for 'The Ghost of You', which had been released a few months earlier to great fanfare. While that song is not explicitly about war, the video was an extremely stylish, harrowing and high-production affair associated with the Second World War and had set a somewhat unattainably high bar for music promos with a wartime background. 'The video is nothing spectacular narrative-wise,' Matt explained to Rockworld TV. 'We had a budget but it wasn't big enough for what we'd envisaged, and My Chem had already done a war video to the point that it looks like a movie, so unless we were going to smash that, there was no point in even dabbling in it. So we kept it simple.' However, the stripped back approach was clearly effective – as of 2015, the video has over 23 million views on YouTube.

With 'Scream Aim Fire' reaching number thirty-four on the UK singles chart and also receiving good airplay on the radio in the USA – not to mention the video being played almost on the hour on every alternative music channel going – the stage was set for a high-profile release of *Scream Aim Fire*: the album. At the end of January 2008 Bullet's long-delayed and much anticipated second album finally got its worldwide release.

Fans expecting an album entirely in the mould of the title track were in for a surprise but, after the opening barrage of 'Scream Aim Fire', 'Eye of the Storm' definitely keeps its foot on the pedal. It was written in a hotel room in LA in the midst of the band's gruelling touring run in support of *The Poison*, after a few drinks had been imbibed: the fast and chaotic nature of the music dictated the subject of the lyrics, which looks at the panic of being caught up in a hurricane.

The most striking feature of the song is the way in which the offbeat guitar riff in the verses interacts with the drumming, creating a turbulent sense of disorder, quite unlike the usual brute power the band trade in. With that said, the song still displays precision in abundance, particularly in the rapid-fire palm-muted riffing in the chorus, which mimics a violent wind tearing across the track.

One of the defining features of the difficult second album is songs about life on the road. Bands who experience a breakout record are most likely going to spend the next year or so on tour in support of it. Come album two, not only are they suddenly under pressure to produce a follow-up in a fraction of the time it had taken to write their debut but their lives since then have been a somewhat repetitive merry-go-round of travelling and performing. It's a catch-22 situation that has made for many a disappointing sophomore record as, while touring in a rock band might be a fascinating life to lead, it's not a particularly relatable topic for the average music fan. 'Hearts Burst Into Fire' could so easily have been Bullet's contribution to the unpopular category of songs about life on the road but they smartly sidestep the clichés by focusing on the much more identifiable themes of missing your loved ones and the joy of seeing them again after a long period apart.

Whereas the opening tracks zero in on classic thrash influences, 'Hearts Burst Into Fire' is new territory entirely for the band. It's still tightly wound and delivered with technical flair but it strips away all of the aggression to let Bullet's pop inclinations shine unobscured. It's a risk that could have so easily backfired were the song not stuffed to bursting point with irresistible melodies and grin-inducing moments. The intro brings with it a luminescent finger-tapped solo that Eddie Van Halen would be proud of; the vocal harmonies in the verse practically beg for audience interaction; the offbeat doubled guitar lines in the pre-chorus fall effortlessly into the chorus; and the middle eight adds pianistic textures the band had never dabbled with before. 'Hearts Burst Into Fire' marks the beginning of perhaps the most defining trait of *Scream Aim Fire* as an album: the division between demonstrably heavy-metal songs – all aggression, lightning fast riffing and screamed vocals – and pop-metal songs. 'Hearts Burst Into Fire' definitely belongs in the latter category but it proves that Bullet do not have to restrict themselves to the heavier, faster, more brutal end of the spectrum to write great music.

But if first-time listeners had any fears that they'd gone soft, the track that immediately follows it is definitely among the heaviest songs on the album, both in sound and subject matter. Called 'Waking the Demon', it's about getting revenge on a school bully 'by slicing pieces off him'; as Matt said to *Revolver*, 'There's some really sick shit in there, so I'm happy.' The song was one of Matt's top three on the album and, as a high-school metalhead – complete with long hair, dark clothes, et al. – he had been no stranger to confrontations at school himself. The song channels the frustrations of the situation, imagining the time when the victim can no longer tolerate it and decides to fight back. In typical Bullet style, the scenario is then accelerated to its most extreme possibility. As Matt sings, 'Those painful times so alone, so ashamed / I'm not coming back, there's nothing to gain'; the torment he's suffered has pushed the narrator so far beyond normal reasoning that it feels like he's possessed by an outside force and he has no intention of fighting it.

Musically, the song wears the band's love of Metallica on its sleeve, particularly in the offbeat fill that Moose uses to bring in the rest of the band. The opening riff and cymbal chokes are one part 'Master of Puppets', one part 'Creeping Death' and all Bullet. Matt's voice is gnarled and throaty – a kind of half-breed between a death-metal scream and a good old-fashioned hardcore roar in the verses – with the chorus opening up into a soaring, power chord-laden bounce. The middle eight is suitably anthemic too, ensuring that the song is nasty enough to get the metalheads in the pit but catchy enough to get everyone else singing along. This is the second track on the album where vocals were heavily cribbed from demo sessions and, once again, the performance is faultless.

The song motors through short, sharp sections with barely a pause for breath. Just as one new riff, melody or vocal line is introduced, it's on to the next, giving the song an irresistible sense of momentum that marries well with the theme of losing control. All in all, it's a practically perfect four minutes of modern heavy metal, equally grimy and polished, both genuinely fierce yet dramatic enough to recall the pomp of metal's glory days. A special mention has to go to Moose, who displays pretty much every technique in the heavy-metal drummer's handbook here, with his feet barely letting up on the double-bass pedal for the entire runtime. Yet, somehow, he never overcrowds the track or stifles the guitars and vocals.

'Disappear' utilises a similar fast, galloping rhythm in the main riff that had been used to great effect on *The Poison*. While the verse feels somewhat workmanlike, rather than genuinely exciting, things steadily build from the stomp of the pre-chorus to the scything two-part chorus, which alternates between a screaming and sung section. The song revolves around a simple repeated two-chord pattern and Jay's bass playing is instrumental in keeping the song moving forward with purpose, particularly in the pre-chorus where the guitars ring out but the bass line keeps moving.

The placement of 'Disappear' on the album is also interesting, as lyrically the song covers much of the same ground as 'Waking the Demon', though with a slightly different emphasis. 'So what's wrong tough guy, why the tears? / You drove me to this, now disappear!' sings Tuck in the song's pre-chorus, where the murderous intent is pretty much carried straight over from the cold and cruel tone of 'Waking the Demon'. But in the chorus an element of doubt creeps in with the line 'Oh God, just what I have become?' The line makes the song work almost like a sequel, as if the narrator who sang 'I'm not coming back, there's nothing to gain' on 'Demon' finds that he can't completely deny his humanity on 'Disappear'. The overwhelming lust for revenge that came on like a possession retreats and what's left is the horror of the killing in all of its ugly reality.

One of Jeff Killed John's final performances, given at the Rhondda Hotel in Porth, circa 2003, with Nick Crandle playing his bass guitar swansong. Note Padge's spectacularly baggy jeans.

Above left: Moose getting his vampire on in Slovenia, 2004. © *Naki/Redferns*

Above right: …Whilst Matt cuts a somewhat less intimidating figure.

© *Naki/Redferns*

Below: Sifting through a set-list with *Total Guitar Magazine*.

© *Jesse Wild/Total Guitar via Getty Images*

Above: Matt, Padge and Moose enjoy a beer whilst hosting an album playback for *Kerrang!* readers in London's famous rock and metal pub, The Intrepid Fox.

© *Hayley Madden/Redferns*

Below: And having almost too much of a good time in a Texas bar, February 2007.

© *Matthew Hyde*

The many faces
of Michael Paget:
Axe-Wielder, Gun-
Slinger, Dirt-Rider.
Taken during the
Scream Aim Fire
sessions, Texas 2007.

© *Matthew Hyde*

Above: The band celebrates winning 'Best British Band' at the Kerrang Awards. London, 2010.
© Getty Images/Brian Rasic

Below: Matt and Padge burn through a duel guitar harmony at the Rockstar Energy Uproar Festival in California, 2011.
© Tim Mosenfelder/Getty Images

Above: Three's a crowd: Jay and Moose goof around as Matt takes a more relaxed stroll back stage in Sydney, 2011.   © *Martin Philbey/Redferns*

Below left: Padge has a great hair day at Reading Festival, 2012.

© *Getty Images/Simone Joyner*

Below right: New boy Jamie Mathias, who went from being a used-car salesman to playing in one of the world's biggest metal bands, takes the stage in Washington.

© *Matt Hayward/Getty Images*

Above: Calm before the storm: Matt finds his chi backstage... © *Martin Philbey/Redferns*

Below: ...And brings the rain in the Windy City (Chicago, 2013).

© *Daniel Boczarski/Redferns*

Long may Bullet's crushing riffs and incendiary songs continue to set the metal world on fire.

'Deliver Us From Evil' deals directly with the vocal issues that Matt was experiencing throughout the recording of the album. Where, previously, the anxiety was giving him writer's block, he was able to turn the issue into songwriting material for the album. But, while musically the song is upbeat, lyrically it drips with depression, frustration and negativity; 'a passion ending, so the world ceases turning' sings Tuck in the chorus, hammering home how the issue was threatening to bring his whole life crashing to the ground. Musically, the song backs off on the frantic riffing that's been at the forefront of the album up to this point and, in its consistently 'pop' approach – particularly the half-time chorus, with its simple chord progression and yearning singing – harks back to the American alternative rock/emo from the first half of the twenty-first century, as typified by Taking Back Sunday, Saves the Day or early Brand New. The spirit of Bullet is definitely still present – most notably in the gang vocals in the pre-chorus – but it's a track that sits more comfortably in the pop-metal vein. Something similar could be said of 'Take It Out On Me', the track immediately following 'Deliver Us From Evil', which, despite beginning with a serpentine guitar riff accented by choked cymbals, moves into an upbeat and structurally simple verse that puts the vocal melody very much at the forefront.

This track also features Benji Webbe of Bullet's pals Skindred, who doubles Matt in the chorus and takes on the second-verse solo. The band had long been friends of Bullet, in the days when Benji was singing with Skindred predecessors Dub War. In fact, when they first made the switch to Skindred, the two bands shared a night out on the town, so it's no surprise that Webbe had eventually found his way to another Bullet guest spot (and it couldn't have hurt that he has one of the most identifiable voices in modern rock). It's his appearance that truly elevates the song, the uniquely honeyed quality of his voice cutting through all the bruising riffs to great effect. The song is also home to a sweeping breakdown – territory the band had not previously explored to any great extent. Built around a chorus-drenched octave bass line from Jay, with an elegantly simple guitar solo and a call-and-response partnership between Tuck and Webbe, it practically begs for the listener to reach in their pocket for a lighter to hold aloft – even if you're listening in your bedroom. And Webbe was more than happy to have seen the lads he had known as eager young hopefuls become fully-fledged heavy-metal contenders. 'I fucking love them all!' he told *The Linc* newspaper when asked about the collaboration and the success of Welsh acts in general. 'Seeing them grow from kids asking me for autographs and photos, to becoming mates and watching them headline massive festivals around the globe. It's amazing how these crap vocalists can get away with it – only joking boys!'

Unfortunately, both 'Take It Out On Me' and 'Deliver Us From Evil', in their less frantic and more pop moments, do allow a little more space for the listener to tune their ear to Matt's vocals. In neither case are they bad; they certainly don't sound like a man with a serious impediment to his voice and, given the seriousness of his condition and the procedure he had to endure, it's something of a miracle they sound so crisp and clear. However, they don't sound quite like Tuck as heard on *The Poison* or 'Waking the Demon'; there's a lack of edge or grit, and, once heard, it's hard not to notice the difference.

Bullet had certainly dabbled in more downbeat, subdued moments in the past – in fact, it had given them their two biggest hits, in 'All These Things I Hate (Revolve Around Me)' and 'Tears Don't Fall' – but 'Say Goodnight' is the closest the band had come so far to an out-and-out ballad. The song is a tribute to Jay's father, who had first fallen ill as Bullet were touring with Guns N' Roses when the band had decided to cancel some Scandinavian shows to allow Jay to spend time with him. The song explores the concept of heaven and the cyclical nature of life itself, as around the time that Jay's dad had passed away he had also welcomed his first child, Abigail, into the world: 'so many colours leave me blind / seeing your face reflect from our baby's eyes', goes the second verse. The song is, by far, the saddest moment on *Scream Aim Fire* and probably the most moving song Bullet had penned to date.

Musically, the song owes a heavier debt to 1980s rock than any other song on the album. It opens with picked chords and a beautifully lyrical solo that begins in the middle register before moving up the neck to a descending arpeggio figure that pops like a firework. And while Bullet had clearly never had any difficulty writing memorable lines and huge, anthemic choruses, they were yet to write anything that could be described as pretty or even beautiful but, in the chorus of 'Say Goodnight', with its overlapping harmonies and delicate hushed delivery, they manage it for the first time (a pattern they would continue on their third LP). The song does kick up a gear into full-on heavy-metal catharsis around the midpoint, with the howls of anguish taking on a particular significance in light of the deeply personal story behind the song.

At this point, it's also worth noting that every track on the album up to this point has featured a guitar lead, performed often by Padge but also at times by Matt, and the range of technical ability on display is highly impressive. From rapid-fire tremolo picking to arpeggio sweeps and huge whammy-bar dive bombs, it's as if both guitarists had absorbed everything that their axe-wielding forefathers had developed before them and incorporated it all into one masterclass of classic heavy-metal guitar playing. The blues-tinged runs on 'Say Goodnight' have more than a touch of Slash about them. There's plenty of Eddie Van Halen-inspired finger tapping, showcased most plainly on 'Hearts Burst Into Fire'. Padge has cited the solo in Pantera's 'Walk' as a particular standout for him, so it's no surprise to hear more than a little of Dimebag Darrell's manic style and saturated tone. Naturally, there are lashings of Kirk Hammett and even a touch of Randy Rhoads's classically inspired elegance. Just one listen to the solos on offer and there is no doubt that Padge is a seriously gifted player.

Interestingly, he has commented that in his first few years after picking up a guitar, he didn't really separate himself from the pack of teenage guitar players around him. 'I think in the last three or four years, that's when I really started to actually learn guitar,' he said to *Ultimate Guitar* in 2006, following the release of *The Poison*. 'I wasted a hell of a lot of time when I was younger.' However, he has since remarked that he practises anywhere from three to six hours a day – after all, you don't pull off those lightning-fast runs without some serious hours of work behind you. And while Matt might not generally be considered the lead guitarist, he is also credited with some solos on *Scream Aim Fire* and proves that he's just as capable a soloist.

The guitar heroics also make an appearance in 'End of Days', a song that was written in Germany while the band were on tour and one of the oldest to make the cut for *Scream Aim Fire*. As Matt explained in an interview with Germany's *Metal Hammer*, the song concerns the end of the world and deciding what you'll do with your last day on Earth. Will you party it away and go as hard as you can knowing that there won't be any consequences? Or will you spend your remaining hours with your loved ones? Musically, the song has all the drama and power that you'd expect from a song about the apocalypse, with the guitar lines kept short, repetitive and savage.

'Last to Know' opens with a harmonised guitar line that screams Iron Maiden but the fierceness of the verse is definitely of a more modern stripe and the song probably comes closest on the whole album to the sound of *The Poison*. It's an unashamedly angry, bitter attack on the band's detractors; those who would find any reason to tear the band down and belittle what they had achieved since the success of their debut: 'Lies you spit are harmless to me / Your spite, your greed, your envy' is the song's rallying cry (or should that be scream?). The song is a relentless assault musically too, the shortest and most frantic sounding on the album. It's great to hear that, despite all their success, the band still had plenty of fire in their bellies and rage in their hearts. There was no risk of Bullet for My Valentine succumbing to mediocrity.

The album closes with 'Forever and Always', which again displays the album's more commercial streak and it's the one that flies closest to the burning sun of pop. Every element of the track is finely tuned for anthem status, from the considerably more relaxed tempo to the simple chord progressions and 'whoah-oh-oh' hook that leaps out of the chorus with the intent to bury itself in your subconscious. Tuck also lets the anger, revenge and bloodshed that's dominated the lyrical themes for the album up to this point go, offering the open-hearted declaration, 'Forget about the shit that we've been through / I want to stay here, forever and always.' It sounds like a love letter to a romantic relationship and it can support that interpretation. But when Matt sings 'standing here in front of all of you,' it's easy to imagine him speaking to the fans that had carried the band this far.

When the band arrived in Texas, 'Forever and Always' didn't exist as a song – the only part that had been written was the song's extended instrumental outro, penned in the back of the tour bus in America. The outro, which repeats the chorus riff over and over with a series of minor embellishments and variations, acted as the basis for the rest of the song, which was written backwards from this point. As Matt noted at the time, it was the most epic song that they had ever written and, in a strange twist of fate, it was only the trouble that Matt had experienced with his throat that allowed the band to finish it at all. The song would become a regular set closer for the next couple of years for the band; a kind of triumphant victory march at the end of all that they'd been through. It's funny how much positivity can come from the worst experiences.

CHAPTER THIRTEEN

FINDING A VOICE

Scream *Aim Fire* was released worldwide at the end of January 2008 and it marked a new chapter for the band. They were the first to admit that they had only got through 2007 'by the skin of their teeth' but, as Matt said to the BBC, 'It was bad, but it's a learning experience and it'll never happen again.' With the album having had such a troubled birth, getting it out into the world must have felt like a huge relief.

Its launch was supported with a series of comic books from writer and illustrator Tom Manning, who created a short strip to accompany each of the eleven tracks on the album. 'Disappear' was a particular highlight, as a bully awakes to find one of his victims has him dangling over a jetty with a weight tied to his ankles – those familiar with the song can probably guess what happens.

Once again reviews were a fairly mixed bag. Some sections of the press just couldn't come round to the combination of yearning melodies and old-school metal. Review website *IGN* said that: 'Bullet For My Valentine and their brethren seem to want the best of both worlds – the hip, indie cred of now and the metal swagger of yore. Much of the time it comes across forced, all-too-ironic and disingenuous. That may not be quite the case here, but it's not far off.' Similarly, interactive ezine *Drowned in Sound* felt the band hadn't developed enough from album one to two, saying, 'Where you would have liked them to open a few new doors in the search to find a sound that was distinctly their own, they appear to have just piled on more Maiden, more Metallica, more Slayer, and a dash of Slipknot drumming.' For others reviewers, though, the album was a marked step forward. *AllMusic* was fulsome in its praise, saying, 'Bullet for My Valentine hits the ground running and maintains a blistering pace throughout most of *Scream Aim Fire* [...] It's definitely harder and more aggressive than the band's debut album [...] and sounds increasingly self-assured and solid for it.' The *NME* called it 'Brit-metal gold', saying, 'that Bullet represent the palatable side of thrash shouldn't be held against them.' And *Time Out* noted that Bullet were now a 'straight-up metal act, rendering them impervious to fashion,' while also commenting that this would make 'crossover success' unlikely.

However, crossover success was just what they were aiming for. Expectations were undoubtedly high for the album but, as first-week sales figures rolled in, it was clear that *Scream Aim Fire* was going to smash expectations. The album had hit number three in the charts in Germany, four in Australia and five in the UK. US results would not come in until a few days later and, while the album actually entered at number four, it had sold just 8,000 copies fewer than the number-one album, Alicia Keys's *As I Am*, which stayed in the top spot for the second consecutive week (in fact, it was at the time one of the lowest sales figures to ever top the Billboard 200). The band were also quick to brush off the naysayers in the media: 'The Poison was picked up to such a degree by the media that there was only one direction they could have gone on this new record – to hate it,' Matt commented to *Westword*. 'There's lots and lots of reviews that have been really, really positive and amazing. But especially here in the UK, the big publications and rock magazines, they've definitely done the predictable thing and slagged it a little bit... It's the only way they can keep articles about us fresh, because we're in there so often, I guess. It's a classic thing. Hype them up, drag them down, build them back up.'

There was no question on the next step for Bullet – to get on the road, in the grand tradition of the hard-working rock band, and tour the album. But there was still a question mark over how Matt's voice would hold up. He had only just got through the recording of the album, so there was understandably some trepidation as to how he would cope playing live night after night. However, Matt had not been idle in his quest to restore the power and durability of his voice. In fact, he had sought the help of the best metal vocal coach in the business – Melissa Cross.

Melissa has spent decades working alongside rock and metal vocalists to ensure that their voices can withstand the unique stressos and strains associated with aggressive vocal styles. However, it wasn't always her plan to be the go-to vocal coach for the world's most famous screamers and howlers. 'I was a singing teacher for about twelve years, something like that, and I had a friend in Connecticut who was producing bands out of his basement,' she explains when asked about how it all began. 'It was an underground kind of genre that wasn't really above the surface very much – a sludgy kind of metal, very fast.' Her friend had a problem: bands would book in the designated amount of time they assumed it would take to record their songs, only to find that the vocalist would not be able to sustain his voice for the duration of the session. 'He wanted to know if I could figure out a way to help his clients get through a session without losing their voice. He brought in the client and I took a listen to it. At first, I kinda freaked out, thought, "Oh my God," but I never took no for an answer.'

Cross's musical heritage stretches back to the 1960s and, while she readily admits she was not a metalhead to begin with, she recognised the spirit of rebellion and emotional honesty in the music. 'I got into music a long time ago, but when I did it was a lifestyle choice. It wasn't about being someone impressive,' she says. 'You were one of them or one of us – part of the counterculture and the underground, or part of the establishment. And metal is like that; it's very real, very pure, very authentic. So even though I don't have any tattoos and I'm not screaming in my own bands, I have a deep respect for it.'

Melissa knew that, if she were to figure out a way to scream safely, she would first have to figure out how to scream herself and then decode exactly what was happening in the body when the scream was produced. 'I figured out a way to make that sound without hurting myself,' she explains, 'and then I went into a physician's office to put the camera into my throat so we could see how you do that.' Many of the clients that she was working with in the early days went on to be highly successful; bands like Killswitch Engage and Shadows Fall – and with their success, her reputation as a vocal coach grew within the metal scene. 'It's a small community, everyone talks, and everyone says, "Go to see her." It was a totally organic thing.'

By the time that Matt was experiencing his trouble, Melissa was already well established. 'Someone once said I've worked with a list of people longer than the line for the toilets at Ozzfest,' she quips, and they were probably right – it's not just the likes of Lamb of God and Cradle of Filth that benefited from her tuition but also the hardcore-punk crowd like Madball, H2O and Sick of It All. She recalls that, from reading about Matt's vocal problems in the press, she was half-expecting to get the call. 'They had cancelled Wembley [supporting Metallica], which must have been the most absolute disappointment of all time. But I knew I'd be able to help him, I just knew it. I thought, "I'm on a mission, I'm gonna fix this guy."' She was flown out to LA from her home in New York and first met Matt as the band were shooting photos that would form the cover and artwork for *Scream Aim Fire*. The vocal lesson was to take place there and then. 'I'd never been on a photoshoot like that, a rock 'n' roll photoshoot,' she explains. 'People were walking around with these fake black crows in this old movie theatre… stylists and make-up people were running around, and I was like, "holy shit!" having to do a voice lesson during all of this.'

Meeting Matt, it was clear that the problems with his voice had taken their toll. 'He was in a really bad place,' she recalls. 'Not angry, not mean, but very down on himself. I know that's how he felt at the time, because I've spoken to him since, and now his whole attitude has turned around. But he was really worried that it was over, and the whole band was worried it was over. They were all thinking, "Shit, this is it, Matt can't do this anymore, and we won't have a job." It was very serious.' However, Cross never wavered in her conviction that she could help the band. As she points out, 'I've fixed a lot of people.'

Matt's first lesson took place right there, in the theatre where the press shots for *Scream Aim Fire* were taken. 'We actually had the stage in that old movie theatre to do the lesson and it was a really cool atmosphere,' she explained. 'We were on the stage where the screen was; it was a very ornate, gothic theatre and we were casting these big shadows in our eyeline. And I was kind of moving my arms like I was casting spells as I went through the exercises – we had fun doing it.'

In fact, there's no magic or enchantments involved in Melissa's teaching, just a bit of science and a lot of technique. As she explains, the trick is to be able to separate the emotional intent of the music from the actual mechanical process of delivering the vocals. 'The biggest challenge is that the music confers a tension and angst, but you have to separate angst from the execution,' she says. 'You have to be able to produce that sound without actually feeling it; it's easy to get carried away.' While the emotions that fuel Bullet's music might be dark, angry and unrestrained, Melissa makes it clear that these emotions cannot be used in the performance if you want to take care of your voice and have to make it last night after night, year after year. 'Obviously you don't want to be a machine and you don't want to be clinical,' she notes. 'You want to be real, but if you get caught up in making it authentic all of a sudden you're using your throat in a way you would with road rage or when trashing your room. And you can't get away with that kind of technique, because that kind of technique will make you lose your voice.'

Ultimately, control is crucial to being a solid and dependable singer. 'People lose their voices because they don't have any control, so the real challenge is to have a kind of controlled chaos going on. You want to confer the chaos and the anger without actually doing it. You have to watch yourself do it so you don't go over the top.' And Matt proved to be a stellar pupil, one whose work ethic and determination was immediately evident to Cross. 'He was a very good student – so good that he recently said to me, "I'm kinda bored of these same exercises, have you got any more?" No one had ever asked me that so I had to make some custom stuff for him, just for shits and giggles.'

Ultimately, what makes a good student of the voice is commitment to getting better. It's not a case of being handed the keys to some secret vault of knowledge and suddenly having all your issues fixed, as Melissa outlines: 'The exercises are simple, but the discovery of the voice happens over time. You keep doing the same battery of stuff over time and it coordinates the way that the vocal cords meet the air, it develops an air supply and it develops the vocal folds that close against the air.' It requires a mind-body connection that not all students naturally have, as Cross explains: 'A warm-up is an awareness of how the voice works. It's not like aerobics, it's not like warming up to run five miles. Your vocal folds are only a tenth the size of the fingernail of the index finger, so it's not athletic. It's more of a mental coordination, and Matt's very good at that.'

Indeed, like many others that have come into contact with Matt, Melissa has come to be very impressed with his discipline and determination to push himself, which she sees as the hallmark of an artist. 'You have to be incredibly focused to be that good,' she points out. 'What he does on the guitar at the same time as singing – there's not many people that can do that. Maybe Robb Flynn [of Machine Head] and a couple of others. The guitar parts are really intricate, and it's very difficult to play something rhythmically oppositional to what you're singing. He does it effortlessly.'

Prior to hitting the road again, other things would need to be different too. The band has never been coy about its love of a drink and there are numerous tales of drunken pranks and booze-fuelled behaviour that surround the Bullet camp. But since the cancellation of the UK tour at the end of 2006, the band had significantly cut down on its drinking, with the rider containing plenty of vitamin-rich snacks and energy drinks as well as booze. Crucially for Matt, the touring schedule would now be compiled with his input, with no shows booked on three consecutive days without his say-so. The exhaustion of constant travelling, jet lag and no rest days between shows had been a key factor in his losing his voice; this way, he would be able to put his health first and ensure there would not be a repeat of the debacle of 2007.

CHAPTER FOURTEEN

TAKE NO PRISONERS

2008 would take Bullet for My Valentine on a world tour but they gave the UK and Europe the first taste of *Scream Aim Fire* in a live setting. The first three weeks of February took the band from an almost hometown show in Newport to London and then on to Germany, Denmark, Sweden and Finland. The tour was not without its issues. Their good friends in 36 Crazyfists were initially booked to support but were forced to pull out after the recording for their new album *The Tide and Its Takers* overran. Roadrunner's Michigan metalcore wrecking crew Still Remains replaced them. Skindred were also out on the road with the band but only managed to fulfil the UK leg of the tour, as drummer Arya sustained an injury while unloading equipment. In a statement, they called the gigs they did play 'the best shows we've played as an opening act in the UK.' The final fly in the ointment came when the very last show of the tour, in Helsinki, had to be cancelled altogether due to illness. Setbacks aside, the tour was a success, with Matt's voice sounding stronger than ever.

During the tour the band were also followed by a camera crew, who captured footage for the 'Hearts Burst Into Fire' video. Superficially, it's your standard supercut of a band on the road, complete with time-lapse traffic, backstage shots, fans going wild and plenty of up-close-and-personal performance footage. It's also a nice document of some of the production they were using on the tour, such as the giant white sheet that obscured the band as they took to the stage, backlit so that their silhouettes loomed over the crowd like ancient spirits. Watch a little closer, however, and it's clear that the song's message of missing your loved ones while out on tour isn't lost. There are plenty of shots of the band looking forlorn on the phone and there's a cameo from Jay's daughter, Abigail, as well as a quick shot of the tattoo he has of her name on his arm.

Jay had been busy with some personal projects around this time. In February, Dear Superstar, a Mancunian metalcore act with a streak of hard-rock revivalism, released 'Live Love Lie', which features Jay providing some back-up screams in the breakdown of the song. This one was taken from the album *Heartless*, produced by Romesh Dodangoda, himself a veteran of the South Wales scene.

The next stop on Bullet's year around the world was the

USA, with the Taste of Chaos tour taking them all the way across the country from the end of February right through to April. The band were looking forward to the stint as they would be out on the road with Atreyu – with whom they had travelled shortly after the release of their first EP – and Avenged Sevenfold. A serious bromance had developed between Avenged and Bullet over various encounters on the festival circuit, with Padge remarking to *Strawberry Daiquiri Music* that 'we've had conversations and we've kind of agreed that we're the same band, but [from] different countries. It's a weird friendship.' Matt, Jay, Moose, and Padge even share matching BFMV/A7X tattoos. As such, the plan for the dates was simple. 'I guess we're just gonna go out and slay as many people as possible and get as many fans,' a clearly excited Moose told *Metal Sucks*. 'Take no prisoners, get on, play, get off, drink like dogs!'

While in America, the band also stopped by Jimmy Kimmel for a performance of 'Scream Aim Fire' and 'Eye of the Storm' on his *Jimmy Kimmel Live Show*. The late-night chat-show circuit in America is a huge channel for bands to be exposed to a mass audience, with over 2 million viewers tuning in to Kimmel's show alone. Since it was the band's first time on live TV, it's no surprise they were a little nervy before it started. Moose, in particular, felt the pressure; despite stating that he'd been fine all the way through rehearsals, he told the official Bullet YouTube channel that, as soon as they went on air, the nerves hit him (in his words, 'I shit my pants'). Still, there are no nerves evident in the performance, with the band headbanging, shredding, grooving and roaring like they were born to do it.

At the stop in New Jersey the band decamped to a local forest to film the video for what would be the next single from *Scream Aim Fire*, album highlight 'Waking the Demon'. The video was directed by Max Nichols, the son of Mike Nichols, who won an Academy Award for *The Graduate*, and it's a very literal but effective interpretation of the song's lyrics. We have the archetypical high-school metalhead (long black hair, Maiden T-shirt, slim build) being tormented by your typical jock (square jaw, blond hair, hot girlfriend). They're making our hero's life hell – soaking him in the shower, beating him with bars of soap – but he's crossing off days on a calendar, hinting that we're headed for the bloodshed that the chorus promises. Sure enough, as he circles 'full moon', he lures the chief tormentor into the woods. To the tune of Padge's manic, discordant solo, he transforms into a werewolf (with a clear nod to classic horror flick *An American Werewolf in London*) and dispatches his victim. There's also a nice stereotype-defying twist right in the video's closing moments, where we see that the bully's girlfriend is not just a heartless witness to the torment but a werewolf herself – and helping the protagonist wreak his revenge.

The vocals accompanying the video and released to radio are, once again, sanitised of a lot of screaming, with Tuck delivering the verse in a more tuneful manner. Despite having previously stated that he doesn't approve of the practice, this PG version of the song is no weaker than the album original.

With its plainly worn classic-metal influence, it actually gives it more of a feel of timelessness. The track was released as a CD single in the States and later in the UK as an iTunes-only release, where it still managed to top the UK Rock chart. It came packaged with an acoustic version of 'Say Goodnight', which translates well to the stripped-back format, despite losing the screaming of the middle eight and the solos.

Unfortunately, the US tour came to an unpleasant early end. In early April, it was announced that Jay was having to fly home at short notice as his daughter had fallen ill. While the band has not elaborated to the press about the details surrounding the incident, it's clear from Matt's statement at the time that the situation was very serious indeed. He told metal news website *Blabbermouth*, 'She's very, very ill, she's in the hospital [...] He had to fly home straight away, which obviously is the correct thing to do, and he wants to be there by her bedside and hopefully she's gonna pull through [...] It's devastating for all of us and we're all very worried.' The band limped on with a guitar tech filling in for Jay at two dates in San Jose and Sacramento, playing an abbreviated five-song set, but it was ultimately decided that they should pull the plug on the remaining dates for the tour. After all, Jay's role in the band was vital, with him taking many of the screamed vocal parts, so his absence would have considerably inhibited the band's ability to do their songs justice.

After a couple of weeks' break, the band were back on tour with Atreyu and Avenged Sevenfold in Australia, this time with Jay back in the fold. While out in Australia, Matt elaborated on the situation concerning Jay's daughter and confirmed that, while it was, indeed, serious, her health was improving and all was now 'cool back home.' He told Australia's *Full Metal Racket Show* that, while the band were keen to press on initially, their thoughts were with Jay while on stage and it 'just didn't feel right.' From Australia the band headed to Japan, where they played four dates over four consecutive days from Tokyo to Nagoya.

Next they dived headlong into a summer dominated by festivals, from Nova Rock in Austria to Fields of Rock in Holland and, of course, the jewel in the festival-season crown – Download. The band once again played the main stage on Saturday, two slots from the top beneath Incubus and The Offspring. They also shared the stage that day with Skindred and 36 Crazyfists so there was, no doubt, some catching up to be done backstage. The band played in front of giant panels of the crows from the cover of *Scream Aim Fire* and played a crowd-pleasing set of their highlights to date; 'Scream Aim Fire' had already firmly planted itself as an explosive opener and 'Waking the Demon' had muscled its way into the set closer position over 'Forever and Always' (presumably to please the riff-thirsty Download crowd).

On 7 July the band flew to Denmark to play the Roskilde Festival, one of Europe's largest festivals, which plays host to some 160,000 people over four days. The event has historically had an eclectic line-up, with a leaning towards the heavier end of the spectrum, but the policy on crowd surfers there is extremely strict. The policy was put in place after a tragedy in

2000 that claimed the lives of nine people when, during Pearl Jam's set, a crush occurred that caused many people to lose their footing. Crowd surfers being carried towards the stage then fell into the space where people had previously tripped and, before they could get up, more crowd surfers were on top of them. It was a horrific and sad incident that sent shockwaves through the music community and has influenced safety and crowd-control policies the world over. It has also led to more than a few ejected patrons, as Bullet discovered.

During their set, people began to crowd surf and, while Tuck states that he didn't incite anything, his feelings were that the crowd had paid for their tickets and were entitled to do as they pleased, so he didn't attempt to stop the crowd either. After the show, the security team approached the band with fistfuls of wristbands that they had cut from fans who had been crowd surfed over the barriers. According to Tuck, it was enough to see the Bullet banned from performing at Roskilde Festival again and, sure enough, they have been conspicuously absent from its bills since 2008. After Roskilde, the band flew to perform at Ruisrock in Finland and, due to delays, almost missed their set, with Jay and Moose pretty much arriving on site and then walking straight on stage.

Bullet's appearance at Reading and Leeds Festivals in 2008 carried a special significance. While they'd played these events twice before, this time they would be the second headliner on the Radio 1/NME stage, directly beneath an iconic Welsh rock act, Manic Street Preachers. Hailing from Blackwood in the South Wales valleys, The Manics had pretty much been

Wales's first bona fide critically and commercially successful rock band. They had opened the way for two other two big Welsh acts in the 1990s – Catatonia and Stereophonics – and, arguably, for all Welsh rock acts after them. The argument could be made that the whole South Wales scene of the late 1990s and early twenty-first century could be traced directly to Manic Street Preachers. In his article for Vice's *Noisey*, Matthew Davies-Kreye of Funeral for a Friend wrote, 'The Manics were very influential on absolutely everyone, whether they admitted it or not. In relation to hardcore, their album, *The Holy Bible*, gave us a license to write music that was as diary-based as theirs. That record was bare and emotional – it was a fucking emo record, really.' There was certainly a sense of occasion as Bullet took to the stage in the tent. Whether they felt it or not, the set was nothing short of ferocious, with Matt's voice, in particular, sounding stronger than ever.

That summer the band also headed out to America for a month-long tour with Black Tide, Bleeding Through and a certain act named Cancer Bats. The latter had released a blistering album entitled *Hail Destroyer* just a few months earlier, which had much of the music press and plenty of music fans positively foaming at the mouth. But it wasn't just first meetings on the tour. Bullet also had the chance to catch up with a very important friend at their show at the Hammerstein Ballroom in New York: Melissa Cross, Matt's vocal coach.

It was nine months after the photoshoot in LA where they had first met and Matt had spent the time wisely, using the exercises and warm-ups Melissa had given him to develop his voice. The difference was marked, as Melissa recalls, and Matt made his gratitude to Cross clear: 'He's such a gentleman, in front of a sold-out crowd he gave me the best shoutout I've ever had. He said, "I'd like to take this opportunity to dedicate this song to Melissa Cross. Without her I wouldn't be here. She saved the band and she saved my career – Melissa this one's for you." I started crying. It was such a nice thing to say.' And it isn't just Matt who was noting the difference that Cross had made – the rest of Bullet have spoken of it too. 'When they talk to the press, at least two of them have said something like, "Matt went to Melissa Cross and she fixed him",' Melissa says. 'They are so openly appreciative about it, and it's so nice.'

Melissa believes that Matt's vocal troubles are behind him – the only thing that remains now is to keep himself interested in the exercises, such is the restless nature of his personality. 'He does his exercises every day, so he doesn't have any problems. His only problem is being bored with them,' she states. 'Every good artist wants to keep pushing the envelope, so they don't get complacent. You mustn't sit and rest on your laurels, you have to keep working. He needs to push the envelope as best he can so it's real.' From Matt's perspective, even after the physical side of his vocal difficulties had been overcome, the mental strain was evident. For months after his recovery he would still step in front of the mic willing his voice to work, the possibility still present in his mind that he would open his mouth and not be able to project any sound, just as had happened in the car park after rehearsal. It was this thought that would keep him on the straight and narrow with his voice.

The *Metal Hammer* Golden Gods and Kerrang! Awards that year had seen the band win a number of nominations. At the Golden Gods they were singled out in the category of Best Album but lost out to a band that they themselves have paid homage to – classic California thrash act Testament, arguably the biggest thrash band outside the Big Four. They had released their first studio album in nine years, entitled *The Formation of Damnation*, to great critical acclaim that year – some luck for Bullet. The 'Scream Aim Fire' promo was also nominated for Best Video but that prize was taken home by Dimmu Borgir for 'The Serpentine Offering', whose video was a tale of a priest abandoning his Christian faith in light of the Crusaders' slaughter of an innocent village. Sometimes you have to accept you've been beaten.

The Kerrang! Awards, however, were a much more successful affair. The band had been nominated for Best British Band, Best Single, Best Video and Best Album; they took home Best British Band. Matt seemed slightly disappointed in an interview with ITV but did insist he'd be keeping his award in the fridge 'with the rest of them'. They could also take some solace that it was their buddies in Avenged Sevenfold who took away Best Album for their self-titled fourth record, which had lived up to the promise of *City of Evil*, while doubling down on the hard-rock influences.

As if there was any doubt as to Bullet's camaraderie with

Avenged, at this time Matt joined the band on stage during Avenged's headline set at the University of London Union for a cover of Pantera's classic 'Walk'. It was this tune that Padge had singled out as being a big influence but Matt proved he's got the grit to fill in for Anselmo's gravelly vocals too.

The end of the year also brought with it a new Deluxe Edition of *Scream Aim Fire*, which came packaged with four additional tracks. The songs were recorded after the main sessions for the album, as Matt explained to the *Metal Hammer* Podcast: 'It's a shame they'll never shine like some other tracks because they're just bonus tracks,' he said. 'It doesn't take a genius to spot the difference between my voice on *The Poison* and *Scream*... something was up. So I re-recorded the songs after my voice got better.'

The first of the four tracks is 'Road to Nowhere', a kind of song of two halves split between an acoustic intro and a fast-and-furious second part. The first half is a perfectly agreeable acoustic emo ballad in the vein of Dashboard Confessional but things really kick into gear at half-time, particularly in the harmonised vocal passage that bridges the two sections. It's a track that fits more in the 'Deliver Us From Evil' vein of *Scream Aim Fire*, built to get crowds singing along, rather than into the pit, but it does so well. 'Watching Us Die Tonight' begins with a riff that recalls Refused's 'New Noise' but develops into a full-on power-metal ripper, with a fantastic single-note vocal line in the verse from Tuck, who delivers his lines in a sinister, almost robotic fashion. It's a song that lets Bullet's classic heavy-metal influences shine bright, with the fingerprints of Maiden and Priest all over the duelling guitars and driving rhythms.

The third bonus track, 'One Good Reason', takes more of a *The Poison*-esque metalcore approach with its syncopated riffing and call-and-response screaming and singing, though it does have a more playful tone than was typical of that album. But it's the last song, 'Ashes of the Innocent', that really stands out from the pack. It's probably one of the heaviest songs the band have ever written, bursting into life without warning with a punishing blast beat and a death-metal growl, before tearing through an exhilaratingly furious verse. The chorus brings things into half-time and, with its harmonised vocal line, has an almost choral feel; it's a complete contrast to the verse, yet provides a beautiful counterpoint to the chaos. The middle eight switches things up again, with Moose instigating a thick, swampy groove under a duelling solo that meets at points in harmonised runs. It truly is a shame that the song isn't given the credence of some of the other album tracks because it's a highpoint for this era, easily standing side by side with 'Scream Aim Fire' or 'Waking the Demon'. (The band did incorporate it into sets around 2009, so it did get some of the airtime it deserved on the live circuit.)

The final tour of the year was to be a run across all of the UK and Europe, taking them from Edinburgh in November to Luxembourg in December (with two back-to-back shows at the Birmingham Academy, due to demand). In support were Black Tide once again, who had, no doubt, impressed with their technically adept fusion of speed metal and pop when they shared the stage on the American tour. Lacuna Coil were main support – the first time the band had been on the road with Bullet since the Rob Zombie incident. On 15 November the band headlined and sold out the Alexandra Palace in London; on the same stage that the likes of Led Zeppelin, The Rolling Stones and The Who had performed, Bullet stepped out in front of over 7,000 people – the largest crowd that they had ever drawn as a headliner.

At first, the band stood only in front of giant stacks of amp cabinets and a banner bearing their name but, as the show developed, the elaborate production revealed itself. Giant balls of flame would shoot up from the front of the stage, light panels to the back flashed in strips like a warning and the band could mount some raised under-lit panels where they were cast in an eerie glow. There was no doubt that this was a heavy-metal show.

Many of the cuts from their debut got huge reactions. The venue was a sea of fists pounding skywards for the intro to 'The Poison' and the roar that greeted the intro to 'Tears Don't Fall' could have shaken the foundations of the historic venue. But it's striking how dominant the material from *Scream Aim Fire* was in the set; the title track opened it and the trio of 'Hearts Burst Into Fire', 'Waking the Demon' and 'Forever and Always' closed it. If there was ever any question whether Bullet would overcome the second-album syndrome, or if the fans would persevere with the band beyond the breakout hit of their first album, the show at Allie Pally certainly put it to bed.

Technically, the guitar work was nothing short of exemplary and Moose drove the set with a mechanical proficiency, never missing a beat in his typically thunderous pneumatic way. As ever, Jay proved to be an invaluable asset in a live setting. It hardly seems fair to call his vocals backing – he seems to draw his screaming up from low in his gut, hunching as he spits his lines into the mic like a wounded animal, the venom and bile dripping from every word. And, just as the band had hoped, the extended instrumental outro of 'Forever and Always' proved an apt closer for a huge headline show, with the 'whoah-oh-oh' hook chanted back by the hall like an ancient folk song.

But the importance of the show is almost lost when you look at it up close. What is most impressive about the performance is the fact that a British metal band – a heavy, brutal, fast, riff-driven, throat-shredding metal band – had taken to the stage of one of London's most iconic venues. They weren't a classic act, cashing in on nostalgia or squeezing a few extra quid from a loyal fan base built up years ago. They had two albums under their belts and they had their eyes set on global domination. Even the mainstream press was sitting up and taking note: *The Guardian* was there and, acknowledging the rabid support of Bullet fans, wrote, 'The kids aren't here to make history, but to live in the moment, which is what makes BFMV's big night so thrilling, and the band's future so bright.' Bullet were now planted firmly front and centre in the limelight and no one could ignore them.

CHAPTER FIFTEEN

LETTING GO
OF THE REINS

fter the triumphant show at the Alexandra Palace, the
band took a month off to recover from the whirlwind
year of touring that had taken them to America, Australia,
Japan and all over Europe more than once. *Scream Aim Fire* had
been a huge hit; today it still stands as the band's bestselling
album, with some 2 million global sales (*The Poison* stands
at closer to 1.2 million; both albums are certified Gold in
the US). They had endured the hardest year of their careers
and their most successful back-to-back and came through
triumphant. But no good band worth its salt can rest easy
for too long. The only way is forward and so thoughts soon
turned to the *Scream Aim Fire* follow-up. They played only one
show in the first three months of 2009 (in aid of the Teenage
Cancer Trust, at the Royal Albert Hall). The Blackout and

Fightstar also joined Bullet at the show and it wasn't lost on Matt that many of his own fans were the age of those that the Teenage Cancer Trust supports (or, as *Time Out* put it, 'The Teenage Cancer Trust continues its ninth year of benefit concerts for young cancer sufferers with a bill that, for once, actually seems to be aimed at the yoof.').

However, attentions in the first part of the year were most certainly on writing new material and, despite how far *Scream Aim Fire* had taken them, the band were starting to feel that it wasn't quite a reflection of where they wanted to be. Bullet for My Valentine had been the target of a huge amount of flak to accompany their meteoric rise to success. Message boards at the time were aflame with heated debates as to whether Bullet were, indeed, the true successors to the British heavy-metal throne, or just young pretenders; whether they had the ferocity and guts of the thrash progenitors that they idolised, or were just emo sheep in wolf's clothing. The press had thrown as much shade their way as it had praise, despite the rock mags putting them on a cover every three months. Bullet had started to feel they'd taken the criticism on board a little too much and it had steered them away from the path they had wanted to tread.

Individually, all members had always been clear that they were not a band that were interested in standing still, and in moving on from *The Poison* they had decided to make a more aggressive, uptempo and 1980s-influenced metal record that would work in a large arena setting. They identified all of the elements that made them unique and pushed them into a more extreme place. But was it where they actually wanted to be? 'Looking back, there was a lot of metal haters saying Bullet for My Valentine are not a metal band and all that sort of Internet nonsense,' Padge told *FaceCulture* when looking back at the album. 'But I think we took that to heart, being new to the game, and thought, "right, let's write a faster, thrashier album, and try and shut them up."' Both Moose and Matt have also stated in separate interviews that they allowed the criticism to cloud their mindset going into the record and pushed to make a heavier album as a riposte to their critics, rather than because that's what they really wanted to do.

There were other aspects of the process that they wanted to change too. All of the songs on *Scream Aim Fire* were written on tour: in hotel rooms, on the back of the bus, pulled together in soundchecks and rehearsals in the spare moments that the band could snatch between their touring commitments. Matt felt it had been a detriment to the quality of the songs. What's more, the whole process had been undertaken with the spectre of Matt's fading voice looming over everyone, which had not only severely hampered the recording process but also affected Matt's confidence and worn away at his overall well-being. 'We weren't extremely happy with the end result,' Matt told *Ultimate Guitar*. 'There's great stuff on *Scream Aim Fire*, but it was never the album it could've been for multiple reasons really. *Scream Aim Fire* was an album we wrote to try to prove people wrong, and wasn't an album we made for ourselves.' The record stands as a testament to where the band were and what was happening to them at the time. But, as of 2011, Matt said that he couldn't listen to *Scream Aim Fire*.

So, with the third album now in the works, things were going to be different. The band set aside big blocks of time to write songs without the distraction of shows to play. 'We wanted to be off the road, in the UK, in a room and writing songs – like we used to,' Matt told *Reverb Street Press*. 'That was the only request this time, to give us the time to write the album... and we did that for about three months.' They headed back to Chapel Studios in Lincolnshire, where they had recorded their debut EP and *The Poison*, hoping to recapture some of the magic from those early days when the band was acting on pure instinct, with no expectations of where their music would take them. This time they were writing with one goal in mind only: 'to be one hundred percent what we are.' No one else was going to have any influence over the sound of the album, not critics, fans or labels. Matt told the *Aquarian*, 'We just wrote like we did in *The Poison* days, we loved it, and we weren't trying to please anyone else but ourselves. So the main objective was to just be happy with what we've written and not try to prove anything to anyone else anymore.'

In the spirit of renewal, the band also decided to consider new producers. They had been delighted with Colin Richardson's work on all three of their official releases, particularly because of his forensic attention to detail when it came to engineering and mixing the sound of the albums. Indeed, the fact that Colin did not get heavily involved in the arrangements or the songwriting process had been a big part of the success of the collaboration. But this time they wanted a producer who had a proven track record of getting involved in that side of things; someone who had a vision for the band's direction as a whole and was willing and able to help the band develop their songs. So, in April 2009, they headed to Malibu to begin sessions with Don Gilmore.

Don Gilmore had got his first experience in the Seattle scene, engineering on Temple of the Dog's first and only record and Pearl Jam's debut *Ten*. But since then he had built his name with American rock bands that had successfully crossed over into the mainstream. His biggest success had been on Linkin Park's *Hybrid Theory*, a short, sharp collection of hybrid pop/rap/metal that distilled and refined everything the burgeoning nu-metal scene had been trying in the early 2000s. The album went on to sell 27 million copies worldwide, making it the best-selling debut in the twenty-first century, and it effectively kick-started an entire (though somewhat maligned) musical movement. Its success and reach were absolutely undeniable, so it's easy to see why Bullet saw Gilmore as the person who could take them to the next level. As Matt said to *Ultimate Guitar*, 'We needed someone who actually looked at the songs, ripped them apart, restructured them, and gave ideas, whereas in the past, we just basically did everything ourselves. We knew we had the potential to be bigger and better, but we needed someone to push us further, and Don was the man for the job really.'

They started sessions at The Document Room recording studios, just minutes from Malibu's Point Dume beach, where the iconic Statue of Liberty scene from *Planet of the Apes* was filmed. It's hard to imagine four South Walian metalheads, tattooed and decidedly untanned, feeling at home in the flashy, ostentatious beach town of Malibu – and the band didn't have much positive things to say about it. 'Malibu is a beautiful, wealthy seaside town [that] sounds great and looks great through a camera lens,' Matt told *Kerrang!* 'But it's basically a few mansions on a hill, a freeway and one shop. There's more to do in Bridgend town centre than the whole of Malibu.' The only upsides were the potential for celeb-spotting, such as when they bumped into Pamela Anderson while buying groceries, and the close proximity to friends – the band hired a car and drove sixty-five miles down the coast to Huntington Beach, home of Avenged Sevenfold, for a reunion with their transatlantic brothers-in-arms.

The sessions were not going well either. The band found that letting someone else in to have a say on their material was harder than they'd expected. After all, it had been the four of them for years and they'd achieved everything up to that point off their own backs, without ever having to consider the opinion of an outside influence. In fact, Matt and Don were butting heads on pretty much everything – the band had walked in with plenty of songs ready to go but now everything from arrangements to lyrics and guitar solos was suddenly up for debate. 'To have someone fuck with something you've created is really difficult to deal with. It was hard for me to let go of the reins,' Matt said to *Kerrang!*, conceding that Don would've been within his rights to walk away from the session, given the amount of resistance Matt was putting up.

According to Jay, much of what was recorded in America ended up being scrapped, such was the degree of discord. By his own admission, Matt's perfectionism was also a key factor in the band's decision to set aside what had been done in California, telling Nikki Blakk's Metal Zone, 'As a metal musician... everything has to be super precise. If I'm unhappy with it, I have to live with that forever. We tried different things, like doing one guitar a side, rather than two, because we wanted to make it sound a little bit different but, when we actually did that, we thought, "This doesn't sound as good as what we've done in the past, so why are we going backwards?"'

Arguments continued between Don and Matt, with Matt walking out of the studio twice in twenty-four hours, turning up at Jay's doorstep to let off steam. 'For the first four months, it felt like we'd fucked up, like we should have done everything on our own,' Matt reflected to *Rock Sound*. The main sticking point was the vocals; the band were more than capable of putting the musical side of things together themselves and Don was happy to let them do so. But Matt's focus was very much on stepping up the vocal performances for the new record. Given what was happening on *Scream Aim Fire*, it was doubtless the area where there was greatest potential for improvement. 'The last record was what it was because I had loads of problems with my throat,' he told *Blabbermouth*. 'But this time, the voice is back, it's firing, it sounds like me again, and I'm really gonna make it a great vocal rock/metal album.' The writing process had shifted accordingly. Rather than writing all of the music in advance and then adding lyrics and melodies after the fact, vocal parts were being composed alongside the music, to better define the songs by the singing. It's a classic pop approach that shifts the emphasis from the riffs to the composition as a whole, ensuring that everything is added in service of the song. Don's expertise is clearly in producing rock records with huge, memorable vocal hooks but Matt found his approach very demanding. 'He was quite brutal when he didn't think something was good enough,' he told *Ultimate Guitar*. 'Whether that was lyrically, melody-wise or performance-wise. He was all about the vocal production.'

Bullet and Don desperately needed a breakthrough and it came when Matt was tracking vocals for a big, melodic anthem, which he compares in tone to 'Hearts Burst Into Fire' and which had already been highlighted as a potential single. Mid-take, he stopped and looked at Don; Matt felt that the song was too commercial, too accessible, and Don agreed. From that moment on, they scrapped all of the obvious, ultra-melodic singles – a decision which was a real turning point in the relationship between Matt and Don. Matt was finally able to let go of the reins to someone who, as he said to the *i heart guitar* blog, 'had sold a shitload more records than me.'

The band decided to continue work on the record back where they felt most comfortable – in their native Wales, where they could be close to family. The band were all still living in Wales at that point. None of them had absconded to LA to live the life of rock stars, so it made more sense for the album to be made in Wales's lush valleys. They decided to finish the record in Monnow Valley Studio: this is the previous rehearsal facility of Rockfield, a hallowed studio that had laid down Black Sabbath, Judas Priest, Motörhead, Queen, Rush and Carcass, among many others. It was also the very place where Randy Rhoads wrote the riff for 'Crazy Train', which Bullet themselves had covered. Perhaps they were hoping to channel some of the inspiration that was clearly in the walls of the legendary space.

It was back in Wales that Matt and Don finally began to gel, with their visions for what the album could be aligning. The main thrust of the sessions was an attempt to streamline the sound. Previously, Bullet had positively stuffed their songs with riffs and counter riffs, thunderous drum parts and raucous vocal exchanges; it was a maximal, bombastic approach. But this time they were very much sticking to a less-is-more principle. 'What we realised with Don was that by stripping things down and making things simpler, it makes it a lot better, a lot more understandable, a lot more listenable and a lot more classic,' Matt said to *Ultimate Guitar*. The pair adopted an approach whereby, if Matt and Don had two different ideas, they would try both, rather than argue. Then, with egos set aside, they would decide with the band what worked best.

Things were going a lot better in the vocal booth too. Matt had found it hard to get in the right frame of mind while in the somewhat sterile recording environment. To a frontman used to singing in front of thousands of baying fans, to get in the right gear to give a great vocal performance while standing in a room the size of a broom cupboard, being stared at through a pane of glass, was not a natural situation. But Matt knew that this was his opportunity to banish all memories of the *Scream Aim Fire* issues. He didn't just want to better that album; as he said to Scuzz TV, he wanted to 'fucking destroy it.' With Don, he worked harder than ever before on the singing parts. Sometimes, they were writing and rewriting the lines up to five times if they were deemed to not pass muster and the work on the vocals took longer than every other element of the recording process combined.

The rest of Bullet were banned from the studio while the vocal tracking was going on. They'd text Matt every day to see if it was done and they were allowed to return but, for days and weeks on end, the reply was the same; he and Don were still working. Martyn Ford and Jeff Rose, who had been so instrumental in producing the demos that would help Bullet get signed, were also present for some of the sessions, no doubt adding to the sense of recapturing the magic of the early days. The result was the strongest singing and songs that Bullet had ever put on tape.

Once recording was complete, it went on to be mixed by Chris Lord-Alge, possibly one of the world's most renowned mix engineers for rock music – the list of his credits includes everyone from Green Day to Nickelback, Avril Lavigne and Paramore. Clearly, Bullet were assembling a team of verified hitmakers to assist in taking them to the next level.

Padge explained his take on Chris Lord-Alge's style to 8747 Production (recording studio) like this: 'Chris's vibe, he just wants everything as wide as possible, as spread out, and he really breathes life into any mix that he does. He's probably the best guy around in the world to mix rock albums, so it was a no-brainer to use him.' And they were completely unabashed in their excitement when speaking to the press. If a band's own opinion is worth anything, it was clear that the record was going to be something special. According to Tuck, even the fact that the band had scrubbed all the obvious, melodic singles from the track listing wasn't enough to dampen the label's enthusiasm for the release. As he said to *Kerrang!*, 'They signed us because they believed that at some point in our career we'd have one record which is a huge, landmark, timeless piece of art, like Metallica did with *The Black Album*. And you know what? I think we've done it.'

CHAPTER SIXTEEN

COMING DOWN WITH A FEVER

Just as recording was being wrapped up on their as yet untitled third record, Bullet hit the road again. In February 2009 the band headed for a gig in Jakarta, Indonesia for the very first time, though the experience brought with it mixed emotions. 'When you're flying in you can see the shanty towns for miles and miles,' Matt told *Metalholic*. 'We got off the plane, [were] ushered through, and escorted to [the] Four Seasons or something. And then you look out the window and across the way there's a kid sitting on tons of rubble and rubbish. It wasn't that it was a horrible place to be, but it felt uncomfortable... it was sad to see kids begging and people sleeping on the side of the road. It made us super thankful for what we do.'

Later in the year, they headed out for the Rockstar Energy

Drink Mayhem Festival in America. Crossing the entire United States over July and August, the tour was headed up by Slayer – the titans of dark, destructive thrash who had formed in Huntington Park, California, in the early 1980s. It was Bullet's first time on the road with Slayer, who were preparing to release what would be their tenth studio album, *World Painted Blood*. Playing just under Slayer on the bill was Marilyn Manson, who was touring in support of *The High End of Low*, his seventh record. With Bullet playing in the third position, it was a dark, heavy and dramatic bill that attracted a serious amount of attention. But behind the scenes, Bullet were greatly enjoying their time with the masters of apocalyptic thrash. Slayer were partying on the BFMV tour bus and, contrary to their none-more-metal image, the boys found them to be thoroughly agreeable tourmates. 'They're very intimidating to look at if you don't know them, but they're pussy cats,' Moose told *SMNnews.com*. 'They're very down-to-earth gentlemen.'

The band premiered material from their new record at the inaugural Sonisphere, where organisers had put together a bill strong enough to get even the most cynical of metalheads' temperatures rising. Metallica and Linkin Park were in the headline spots, with Lamb of God, Mastodon, Machine Head, Avenged Sevenfold and Alice in Chains also billed. The festival was held across six European venues, with the UK stop headed to the legendary site at Knebworth House, which had previously hosted everyone from Pink Floyd to the Rolling Stones, Frank Zappa, Led Zeppelin, Deep Purple,

Queen and Dire Straits. It was a fitting setting for the band to launch Bullet version 3.0.

'We wanna play you a new fuckin' song right now. How does that sound?' Tuck asked the crowds and, judging by the roars, they thought it sounded good. 'Obviously, you don't know it… which is good for us, 'cause if we fuck up, we don't look like dicks. But that doesn't mean you can fucking stand still, take fucking video footage and put it on YouTube tomorrow.' (You can, in fact, view the video on YouTube.) The song they played is what would come to be known as 'Pleasure and Pain', although the lyrics and melody are completely different. It's interesting to hear a work in progress. As Matt said, vocal parts were sometimes rewritten up to five times and, as perfectly serviceable as this version is, it lacks the punch of the version that finally makes it to the album, where practically every line is a precisely written hook. But, just as Bullet had been promising in interviews, it was fast and heavy, yet somehow streamlined, stripped of unnecessary embellishment. This was a leaner, meaner Bullet, poised to take themselves to the next level and the new track had got tongues wagging. 'It's not thrashy or really intense metal or anything. It's just like a mid-tempo kind of really nice, hard rock song,' Matt told the German version of *Metal Hammer*. 'I don't even class it as metal, really. It's got metal influences and a really cool metal riff, but the song, as a vibe, is more hard rock.'

Despite it being a successful outing for Bullet, the festival was beset with cancellations – Fear Factory, Frank Turner and

Thin Lizzy all had to pull out and Machine Head almost did when the addition of Limp Bizkit pushed them down the bill. (They ultimately ended up playing a special-guest slot on another stage.) The festival also has the sad honour of being the last show that Jimmy 'The Rev' Sullivan – drummer of Avenged Sevenfold – would ever play with the band. He died in his home on 28 December that year, the result of an accidental overdose of prescription drugs and alcohol, possibly exacerbated by an undiagnosed heart condition, aged just twenty-eight. It wasn't just his technical flair and showmanship that Avenged would miss. He was also a vocalist and writer for the band, contributing to many of their best-known songs. His funeral was held in Huntington Beach in 2009 and Matt was in attendance, less than a year after he had visited while taking a break from recording in Malibu. Avenged's guitarist Synyster Gates, who had known Jimmy since childhood, delivered the eulogy. '[It's] devastating for the guys, a very sad time,' Matt commented to Zane Lowe on Radio One. 'Hopefully, they've got the strength to carry on.'

Summer 2009 also brought with it awards season and Bullet, once again, found favour at the Kerrang! Awards. Hosted by Slipknot's Corey Taylor and Scott Ian of Anthrax, the band picked up the prize for Best British Band for the second year in a row. In October Padge also cemented his status as a renowned guitarist with the release of his own instructional DVD, showing how to play Bullet riffs and solos and accompanied by his typically laconic commentary. But with the rest of the year taken up with completing the record, the band kept extra-curricular duties to a minimum and little was heard from the Bullet camp for the remainder of 2009.

The engines on the Bullet war machine roared into life once more in 2010, when the new album was announced – the title would be *Fever* and the first song to be released was 'Begging for Mercy'. Slick, heavy and incredibly dark, excitement in response to the track was immediate; Zane Lowe premiered the song on his Radio One show, playing it twice, back-to-back. It was shortly followed by the release of the first single to promote the album, 'The Last Fight', which dropped alongside a video directed by Paul R. Brown. The track was classic Bullet, beginning with a thunderously fast palm-muted riff that opens out into ringing chords. Tightly wound but with a sense of scale and grandeur, you feel from the opening bars that it's a riff that could fill an arena. Before you've had time to catch your breath, another is brought in to underpin the verse and it's here that the influence of Gilmore becomes clear. The verse vocals feel chorus-like; the phrases are simple, yet placed neatly within a musical setting that's more spacious and crisp than the usual frantic assault of riffs and counter-licks. Even the solo is based around a repetitive melodic phrase that works more like an instrumental passage than an out-and-out fret-melting lead; its purpose in the song is to develop and add variety to the musical ideas that have already been introduced, rather than to demonstrate the skill of the player.

Clearly, the band had taken Gilmore's lessons to heart and

the result was a more controlled, mature-sounding Bullet. But the most notable change is in Matt's voice. From the perfectly placed harmonies to the emotive pre-chorus and the stirring, driving chorus where Matt breaks into a gravelly register, it's clear that Matt is 100 per cent back on form, brimming with confidence and power. There's also significantly less screaming than we'd been used to from Bullet; the song still has its aggressive vocal moments but they're used sparingly as the song careers towards its climactic final moments. You'd have expected some grumbles that the band were sanding down their rougher edges to appeal to a bigger audience but, in reality, Bullet had never been coy about their desire to claim the biggest audience that they possibly could and *Scream Aim Fire* had already been moving towards a more seamless fusion of pop and metal. 'We're bringing it to a whole mass of people who wouldn't have given a shit before we came along,' Matt noted to *i heart guitar*. 'That sounds maybe a little bit arrogant, I know, but it's a fact!'

The song was written at Chapel Studios during the two weeks that the band decamped there to write and, as is often the way with great songs, the instrumental part came together very quickly, in under an hour. The band jumped into the live room to record a demo and, rather than multi-track it, they were so caught up in the moment that they recorded it live. That night, after several drinks had been consumed, Matt jumped into the vocal booth and recorded a scratch vocal. The only thing that changed from the booze-fuelled demo version to when the final version came to be recorded in Wales is the middle eight.

Lyrically, the song explores the challenge of addiction and it's a topic that the band had spoken on before but never directly addressed with their music. And while rock 'n' roll is no stranger to first-hand reports of drug abuse, 'The Last Fight' is written from the perspective of someone dealing with a loved one who is an addict. 'Cold sweats, hallucinations / I wanna scream to show the hell I'm going through / The addiction's taken you'; the lyrics make it clear that an addiction is equally as destructive for those around as for the sufferer and yet the chorus is a rousing plea not to give up on a drug abuser, to fight as hard as you can for one last time to save them from themselves. It wouldn't be fair to say that rock and metal, in general, condone drug use – though there are some artists and songs that plainly do – but in even the most sordid account of the horrors of drug abuse, a musician runs the risk of glamorising addiction, of making it look like a crucial accessory in the life of a tortured artist. Indeed, western culture has a tendency to push musicians into the role of martyrs who must suffer hardships to justify the seriousness or weight of their art. As such, it's refreshing to see Tuck look on the well-worn subject from a different angle and represent the experience of people that the standard addict-artist narrative usually overlooks.

The truth is that no fan could have been unhappy with the new, refined version of Bullet as presented in 'The Last Fight' because it contains everything that made them great in the first place: a bone-crushing thrash riff, the melodrama of 1980s hard rock, a huge pop chorus and flawless musical performances across the board. The removal of extraneous details only served to highlight the band's strengths better.

Paul R. Brown's clip that accompanied the release was shot in LA. The concept is simple: a performance video interspersed with shots of a boxing match where a fighter battles a masked opponent. At the climax of the video, it's revealed that the masked pugilist is the same person as the other fighter: an analogy for the struggle of a drug problem – you are in conflict with yourself. In stripping back the story element that had been the focus of previous promos, the video sends the same message as the song. This is a leaner, meaner Bullet, unburdened by unnecessary extras. It's an undeniably stylish clip too, with the band shot in a cold and grimy light with a camera that zooms in and out of focus, restlessly panning as they play. Matt was delighted with the video, feeling that Brown had made the band look more like a unit than ever before. 'He makes bands look like rockstars,' he said to the official BFMV YouTube channel. 'It was weird watching it back, 'cause we actually looked like a band... we never think of us as that, we're just four friends that rock out together and always have done. We look like rockstars for once, rather than idiots.'

With 'The Last Fight' warmly received by fans and the press alike, the stage was set for the release of *Fever* on 26 April 2010. The album opens with a track that could have quite easily not made the cut; with the record pretty much finished, the band had a single day left in the studio and Matt and Moose decided to play around with one of their favourite riffs that hadn't yet found a home. That riff was the hammer-on lick that runs like a river of tar through the black-as-night 'Your Betrayal', a track that was written in an hour at the last moment and, no doubt, cried out to be included in the final line-up. The opening salvos of snare and muted guitar are crushingly heavy in their simplicity and, paired with the more restrained tempo, the song has a virulent groove. The verse utilises the quiet/loud dynamic that the band had employed on the likes of 'Tears Don't Fall' but, where the tone of that was emotive and angsty, 'Your Betrayal' is austere, cold and cruel. Lyrically, we're back in similar territory to that of *The Poison*; that of spoiled love and a narrator with revenge or murder on his mind. Matt uses every trick in the book to infuse the words with menace: he whispers, screams and explores the upper limits of his tenor range, so it's not just the theme that recalls *The Poison*; his voice has the strength that we heard on that album too.

But the song's best and most surprising moment comes in the middle eight, when the band settles into a swampy, lurching rhythm while Matt sings a wordless vocal hook that's mysterious and seductive in equal measure. They'd proven many times over that they could write catchy hooks but this shows a whole new side of them; one that's willing to explore other moods and textures and not afraid to kick a song in a new direction. Whereas much of Bullet's material prior to this point had been positively overflowing with emotions, riffs and rhythms, as if the band were constantly adding to songs until they were overflowing with ideas, 'Your Betrayal' has a restrained tension. It's a song that displays more of a 1990s influence than the band had previously shown; it has the kind of gloomy power of Alice in Chains.

The title track comes next and, whereas 'Your Betrayal' is heavy in both sound and tone, 'Fever' is an unashamed party track. Written at Monnow Valley and one of the last songs to be written for the album, it's a song about excess, lust and cutting loose and, for Matt, it was the boisterous tone of the music that dictated the lyrical direction. Bullet had written about sex before, usually with a morbid undertone. But the desire in 'Fever' is as unfiltered as it comes: 'Come here you naughty girl, you're such a tease / You look so beautiful down on your knees,' sings Tuck in the middle eight. It's the first time that the band had attempted to write such a straight-down-the-line party song but, thanks to the exuberant riffing and ultra-catchy pre-chorus and chorus, it works perfectly.

The chorus for the track was lifted wholesale from an old scrapped song and, instrumentally, it yet again displays the band's new intent to let the vocals lead the music – the riffs are more spacious and simple to allow the vocal parts to shine. While the breakdown is clearly designed to get audiences engaged, with a bass-drum beat carrying through that begs to be clapped along to (preferably with hands aloft), the song once again shows that the band are willing to let go of some of the trappings of classic metal that had so defined them in the past. While the main riff screams power metal all over, there's no wailing guitar leads to speak of; it's a hard-rock song powered by a big catchy vocal and all the more effective for it. As the band has said in interviews, the new approach was to do what was best for the song and no more, not what was best for the individuals. With the song representing a fresh new direction and indicating where they might want to head in the future, the decision was taken to name the whole album after 'Fever'.

After 'The Last Fight' – the final track in a pretty much flawless opening trio that puts the album on an incredibly strong footing – *Fever* eases off the pace with 'A Place Where You Belong'. Essentially a mid-tempo rock ballad, it's the most obvious claim the band has made for crossover success to date. But, while the song holds back on the aggression, it ups the ante in terms of arrangement and songwriting sophistication. Dynamically, it fits into the same category as the likes of 'Tears Don't Fall' but there's a lot more to get to grips with musically, from the rising and falling verse to the superb vocal line that carries through the chorus and the two guitar solos. There's also a definite restraining hand on the distortion pedal, with the band happy to linger in yearning ballad territory. If this was Bullet doing exactly what they wanted to do, they were showing that they no longer needed to prove how fast, heavy or hard they could play – they could do half as much as they did on *Scream Aim Fire* and be twice as powerful.

But one thing that hadn't changed was Matt's willingness to take himself to dark places to come up with lyrical content. 'A Place Where You Belong' imagines not being able to clear the air with an estranged loved one before they pass away and having to live with the burden of things unsaid for the rest of your life. 'It's about losing a loved one before you make amends with them,' Matt told *Music Photocalypse (musicalypse. net)*. 'In the song it's more of the sense of a relationship, but it could be with a parent, a friend or someone you've had a hard time with and you don't talk for years and then they pass away and you've never made that connection.' Tuck's lyrics had sometimes faced criticism for lacking subtlety but he has to be commended for his willingness to travel to the extremes of his imagination and tackle unpleasant thoughts in his writing. 'A Place Where You Belong' took one of the longest stretches of time to write of all songs on the album and changed significantly from its very first demo version to the final cut. However, it wasn't unusual for the band to have to sit with the slower, more downbeat numbers for longer, to let them develop at their own rate until they took their final shape. The result, in this case, was one of Matt's favourite songs on the album and certainly a high point in terms of commercial viability.

But Bullet weren't about to hand in their metalhead membership cards just yet. 'Pleasure and Pain' delivers a muscular punch of heavy metal, with a brutal scream that announces the introduction of a simple yet pulverising riff, which drives the whole song. The band had first played 'Pleasure and Pain' on the Mayhem tour in America and had a near complete version ready to take into the studio that they had got comfortable with over six weeks. But, upon playing it for Don, they soon discovered that he wasn't particularly impressed with the vocal parts, so the singing was scrapped and rewritten completely. (The band have even mentioned the YouTube videos of the previous version, reassuring fans that the multiple versions represent value for money.)

The result is a much stronger hook in both the verse and chorus and a strong track in the classic Bullet vein that keeps the momentum going through the middle of the record. The whole song is largely designed around one riff and two chords but is no weaker for its direct approach. In fact, it feels heavier for delivering exactly what is needed and no more. The song originated from a drum beat that Moose had played, which caught the ear of the rest of the band and from which the main riff was developed. While Matt insists that the riff is, in fact, very easy to play, it sounds agitated and frenzied. And for fans of Bullet's athletic guitar playing concerned that they might be moving away from solos, the middle eight comes complete with a guitar break that leads into a ripping lead part. They might have learned when to take their foot off the gas but they still knew the right time to put the pedal to the metal too.

Matt himself has stated that the next track, 'Alone', is one for the musos. But you don't have to have any knowledge of the techniques of writing and playing music to appreciate what is one of the strongest songs the band had written to date. It opens with an unashamedly epic instrumental, where huge power chords ring out under a finger-tapped solo accompanied by stabs of synthesised strings. It recalls the opening riff of 'Hearts Burst Into Fire' but, where that song maintained the stirring tone throughout, 'Alone' quickly discards it and veers into unexpected territory. The song is truly impressive – there's a series of equally exhilarating riffs that link together beautifully, powered by a straight-down-the-line beat from Moose that ensures the song has a backbone of iron. But none of the technical wizardry ever gets in the way of the song, with the vocals always in the spotlight. Even the key change that ushers in the double lead solo in the middle eight feels completely natural and the string parts sitting in the background work wonderfully well to add to the scale and grandeur of the song.

At the five-minute mark, the band have already thrown enough at the track to make up about three songs if it were deconstructed but the glorious intro returns once again to drop the curtain on what is surely the band's most prodigious moment. It's the best example they have of incorporating dozens of musical ideas into one composition while never straying from the feeling of it being an effective, solidly constructed pop song: it's Bullet's Abba moment. Lyrically, Matt is venting his spleen again, dreaming of the death of someone he hates, as he had many times in the past. It's unashamedly vitriolic – 'you can die and rot alone', is the song's most repeated line – but when contrasted with the electrifying arrangement, it makes for an effective one.

'Breaking Out, Breaking Down' had been written well before *Scream Aim Fire* was released and existed as an almost complete instrumental demo. While Matt was in the midst of the vocal session at Monnow Valley Studios in Wales, he began skipping through tracks on his iPod and came across the recording. Who knows why the band opted to put it to one side all those years ago, or what Matt heard in the demo this time round that he missed the first time, but he immediately went to the others and suggested they record the song officially. For lyrical inspiration, Matt dwelled on the theme of escaping your everyday life, overcoming adversity and pursuing your own path, and the song was born.

There's no doubt that the piece fits better here than it would have on *Scream Aim Fire*, as the spacious, mid-tempo musical approach leaves plenty of room for a scene-stealing vocal performance, which is exactly what Matt delivers – and, given his vocal troubles, wouldn't have been able to in 2007. Aside from a particularly pretty acoustic outro, the song doesn't have a whole lot to distinguish it among the particularly strong pack on *Fever*. It is by no means a misstep and will certainly have its particular admirers among Bullet fans. But on an album of highly distinctive tracks, each with its own tone and direction, it serves best to carry the album into its exceptionally strong closing section.

'Bittersweet Memories' is a full-on power ballad, closer to the blueprint of the form than the band had ever gone before. There are no punishing breakdowns or brutal riffs to temper the melodrama, as with 'Say Goodnight'; it is pure 1980s sentimentalism and works all the better for it. Plenty of their previous output had concerned the chaos and turbulence of a bad relationship, as 'Bittersweet Memories' does, so, lyrically, the song does not push the envelope for Bullet. But in writing an unashamed ballad, the band finally exposes a soft side that every fan always knew was there. And, as far as ballads go, it's great: the verses are based around repetitive phrases that frame the dying relationship in new angles so within a couple of lines you're able to hum along and after a couple of listens you can sing along. The music to the song had to be rewritten a number of times to better work with the vocal line and it was right to do so, as its radio appeal is immediately obvious. The chorus is huge, though Bullet had long since proved they were capable of writing those. Perhaps the song's biggest surprise is that it doesn't contain a guitar solo in the typical sense. If Bullet were simply following the template as written by the masters of the form – Whitesnake, Heart, Poison – then they would have been sure to include one but its omission shows that the band really were writing for the song and not for the sake of it. This one has theatre, pain and a tale of love lost. It is everything you want from a ballad but delivered with Bullet's raw edge and it's exactly what *Fever* needs.

'Dignity' is another mid-tempo track that first reveals itself as more hard rock than metal, moving from a riff that carves like a knife through to a more bouncing, punk-inspired verse and an emotive rock chorus. It's an odd combination of contrasting passages that somehow work together brilliantly – a capability Bullet had shown off many times before – and by the time the band switches gear into a full-on thrash middle eight, you're so completely carried along in the momentum that it's easy to overlook how they've mashed three different genres together. 'Let them put us down, hope we're not around / They pray we go away, but we're here to stay,' sings Tuck; it's another middle finger to the critics and the naysayers who continued to trash the band. By this point, they were all well aware of their status as a love-or-hate act – they'd addressed it before on 'Last to Know' from *Scream Aim Fire* – but had clearly not lost any of the fire in their guts when it came to sticking up for themselves. But where 'Last to Know' practically drips with resentment, bitterness and frustration, the message of 'Dignity' is positive. It's not about attacking those that would seek to tear you down, it's about living your life the way you want to in spite of them. As the chorus goes, 'Don't push me 'cause I won't go quietly / I'd rather die with dignity.' Accordingly, it's one of the most uplifting choruses the band have ever written.

Given Bullet for My Valentine's meticulousness, it's probably not a coincidence that the album's most inspiring track lies next to its darkest. They know exactly how to give you what you need when you need it and 'Begging for Mercy' gives you brutality in spades. It's another track that was written in Chapel Studios, where the band had set up to capture a little of *The Poison*'s spirit, and it wouldn't sound completely out of place on that album. Musically, it's quintessential BFMV, with big metal riffs, watertight drumming sprinkled liberally with double kick-drum accents and a huge chorus with harmonised vocal line. But it's no weaker for following the template Bullet had set in 2006. If anything, it shows how far they'd been able to refine their classic sound and it's the utterly merciless vocal performance that takes the song from being another Bullet banger to one of the best and heaviest songs they had ever written. The delivery of the line 'drain your blood / watch it pour' is enough to keep meek listeners up at night.

But only a no-holds-barred performance in the booth would do justice to the content of the song, which is perhaps the most extreme place that the band have dared to venture. It all started with Matt and Jay playing a game of pool. Since the track was so brutal, they knew they were going to have to go somewhere heavy with the words too, so they started challenging one another to come up with sick ideas. What would you do if someone harmed your family, they asked one another – if someone murdered your partner? The resulting violent fantasies formed the content of 'Begging for Mercy', which centres around a killer imprisoning his victim in the basement and bleeding them from the heels. Believe it or not, the band have stated that they actually had to tone the lyrics down to get to those that you hear on the record.

'Pretty on the Outside' concerns something that almost everyone can relate to – a relationship with someone who's beautiful physically but ugly in nature and they don't mince their words about it – 'Now I fucking hate you with all of my heart,' Matt spits in the second verse, with enough venom to melt the music around it. The song again has something of a 1990s flavour, recalling 'Your Betrayal' in its gloom. The pre-chorus is particularly powerful – Matt uses an as-yet unheard part of his voice, a kind of desperate howl that embodies all of the song's despair and self-loathing before launching into the final huge chorus of the album. Recording the track posed problems; the song is in 6/8 time signature, rather than the standard 4/4, meaning that beats per bar are counted in two multiples of three, rather than one multiple of four. According to Matt, Moose couldn't get his head around the timing and lost his temper in the studio but, fortunately, persevered to ensure the track got finished.

Taken as a whole, *Fever* hangs together better than both *Scream Aim Fire* and *The Poison*. *Scream Aim Fire*, in particular, had suffered from a slight patchiness, as if the band were caught between two different visions of where they could be: the out-and-out metal band or the pop-metal fusioneers. As such, they ended up falling in the crack between the two. But *Fever* suffers from no such uncertainty. There is no seam visible between the metal and mainstream-rock facets of their sound; they are integrated to the point that they are inseparable.

It is also a remarkably confident effort that's consistently strong from beginning to end, proving that they could write dark and angry music that is also catchy, memorable and radio-friendly. It expands the borders of where the band had taken their music, introducing new textures, tonal palettes and emotions, while simultaneously stripping back and distilling the core elements. And crucially, it proved that, when Matt's voice was firing on all cylinders, he had the power and flexibility to be one of metal's most recognisable frontmen.

Matt had identified *Fever* as BFMV's *The Black Album* and it's a comparison that bears weight, not just for the notorious studio fallouts between Metallica and producer Bob Rock. That, too, was an album that developed Metallica's sound without complicating it and which proved a metal band did not have to be constrained by how heavy they were or how fast they used to play. 'This record's diamond-tipped tuneage stripped the band's melancholy guitar excess down to melodic, radio-ready bullets and ballads,' wrote *Spin* magazine of that album. They are words that could easily have been written about *Fever*.

There were certainly plenty of positive noises in the press about the success of *Fever*. *Kerrang!* hailed the album as a career best, giving it a five-K review and writing that the 'inspired songwriting, impeccable musicianship and unbridled confidence propel Bullet to a level that they could only point towards previously.' *Rock Sound* noted the influence of Gilmore in producing a melodically driven record that steers away from the band's original metalcore sound, whilst also noting, 'You get the feeling that although there are fewer nods to their thrash-favouring past, Bullet for My Valentine are being more honest than ever in creating a melodically based record that still provides moments of heavy.' Writing for the BBC, Raziq Rauf called it an 'outstanding set of songs,' *AllMusic* said it was 'a solid disc by a group that knows its own strengths' and Q *Magazine* said the sound had been 'polished until it gleams like chrome.' While it was by no means a clean sweep – the album still found its way to the ears of Bullet's detractors, who then found their way to their keyboards – they were easily the most favourable reviews the band had received in their career. In moving towards a more melodic and classic sound, Bullet had played to their strengths and come out victorious.

CHAPTER SEVENTEEN

AREnA
COnQUERORS

The album was released on 26 April 2010 and first-week sales were stellar, shifting 71,000 copies in the US, debuting on the Billboard 200 at number 3 and topping both the rock and alternative charts. It was Bullet's best charting album in the US, helped along by the release of the video for 'Your Betrayal', which had been shot alongside the video for 'The Last Fight' in LA. Again, it was a simple, performance-led video, this time accompanied by visuals on the theme of the seven deadly sins and with plenty of fire, as if to prime new fans on what to expect at a Bullet live show. The album also cracked the top five in Australia, the UK, Japan, Germany, Austria and Switzerland.

Promotion began with a secret London show on 29 April. It was the first time that the band had played in the UK since Sonisphere in 2009 and fans were camped outside the venue – which turned out to be the Islington Academy – from the early hours to catch *Fever* live (no pun intended). The following day the band headed to the BBC's Maida Vale studios to record a live session for Zane Lowe. In the interview, they revealed that they were all nursing hangovers from the night before, with the exception of Matt, who was tired for an entirely different reason. On 25 March, Matt's partner Charlotte had given birth to the couple's first child: a baby boy who they named Evann. Moose and Jay already had children of their own and the forthcoming tour was to be the first time that Matt had experienced leaving a little one behind. He was understandably nervous. 'I am trying not to think about it right now, because I don't know how I am going to react,' he told the *Aquarian*. 'I can't see it being a happy day. Even though it's going to be exciting, we get on a plane and go to the United States and play live every night, which is awesome and what we love; having a kid has turned my life upside down a little bit. It's going to be a day of very mixed emotions, but it's going to be something I have to do. I am not the only guy that has to do it, other musicians, policemen, soldiers, so I am not the only one.'

Matt has been very outspoken about the effect that Evann has had on his life, saying that his birth completely re-prioritised his life. Out was the reckless lifestyle of a touring rock musician and in was a newfound appreciation for his family, his partner and his health. But where many musicians are quick to baulk at the prospect of their child following them into music, Matt was keen on the idea. After all, he had a lot of wisdom to impart.

The summer was heavily dominated by festival slots, with the band playing the second Sonisphere, Download (where they headlined the newly named Ronnie James Dio stage, following the legendary singer's death from stomach cancer in May), Nova Rock in Austria, Metaltown in Sweden, Graspop Metal Meeting in Belgium, FortaRock in Holland and Bilbao BBK Live in Spain. A particular highlight was the Greek leg of Sonisphere, where Bullet played on the same bill as Metallica, Slayer, Anthrax and Megadeth – the first time ever that the Big Four had played on the same bill. Fans had been demanding it for years and the bands seemed almost as incredulous as everyone else that it had never happened. As Slayer's Kerry King told *Blabbermouth*, 'It's about fucking time this happened, and about time the fans finally get what they want.'

Following on from the positive critical reception of *Fever*, that year's awards season also proved to be lucrative. At the Golden Gods, they won the Best UK Band award, although weren't on hand to personally accept it (Bullet's pals Skindred, however, did perform at the ceremony, ensuring that someone was in attendance to keep the spirit of South Wales alive). At the Kerrang! Awards, hosted by Slipknot's Corey Taylor and Anthrax's Scott Ian, Bullet were the most successful band of the night, taking home both the Best British Band and Best Live Band awards (though they lost out on the Best Album award to Paramore's *Brand New Eyes*).

Bullet were in attendance to pick up their awards and seemed particularly surprised by the Best Live Band win – 'Fuckin' 'ell, I thought fuckin' Muse would have had it if Muse were fuckin' nominated,' began Moose's acceptance speech.

September saw the band on a headline run around Australia and then on to the US, which sadly brought with it the odd hitch – the show in Providence on 5 October had to be cancelled due to Matt's illness and then, on 8 October, Jay once again had to leave the tour to attend to a family matter. The band's bass tech, Calvin Roffey, this time stepped in to fill Jay's shoes. Roffey is himself the bass player for The Smoking Hearts, a rough-and-tough hardcore band dipped in rock 'n' roll excess, so live duties were not new territory for him. (Two years later, Jay and Moose would personally recommend The Smoking Hearts to *Rock Sound* as a band to watch, describing them as 'Motörhead on more speed, beating up the Anti-Nowhere League then bumming The Ramones.') In an interview with Hertfordshire newspaper *The Comet*, Roffey revealed that it was the illness of Jay's new baby boy that had forced him to head home. Not wanting to cancel more shows, the band asked Roffey to learn the set and step in. He also explained why the larger crowd didn't intimidate him: 'I wear glasses and when I'm on stage I can't wear them so it didn't appear that there was that many people,' he said. 'I didn't really notice there was a big crowd, it was just the amount of stage I had to fill.' Fortunately, Jay was back in the fold by 18 October.

Unsurprisingly, 'Bittersweet Memories' got the nod to be

the next single and was released accompanied by a video shot by Shane Davey. The band decamped to the abandoned Oriental City shopping centre in north London to shoot the moody post-apocalyptic clip, which sees the band walking the deserted halls, going hell-for-leather at a trolley with a bat, singing in the rain and generally trying to shake off thoughts of an attractive blonde ex-girlfriend who keeps cropping up. As the director explained, it's a visual landscape that parallels the emotional tumult of the song and it's got all of the darkness and drama you'd want from a video to a rock ballad (Guns N' Roses' 'November Rain' being the high watermark that inspired dozens of similar shoots – notably 'Seize the Day' by Bullet's good friends, Avenged Sevenfold).

But the big news of the year was the headline tour in the UK that would bring 2010 to a close. The band had made no secret of their arena ambitions right from the very start. Indeed, in 2006 Padge was asked where he'd like to see the band in 2010 and his response was to be playing arena tours, with all the bells and whistles in terms of pyrotechnics and production that typically accompany them. The band would be embarking on their very first headline arena tour from 6 to 13 December – so Padge's dream came true, with just eighteen days to spare. The tour would take them from the Birmingham NIA to the Manchester MEN, Glasgow SECC, Cardiff CIA and, finally, the iconic Wembley Arena. *Fever* had done it; it had carried the band into the big leagues. They had spoken of wanting to be the torch bearers of heavy metal; to be seen as the next in line to the crown after the likes of Maiden and Metallica. Finally, it felt as though they were getting there.

When it came to the week of shows, Padge was the first to admit he was 'bricking it'. 'I think it was all down to the scale and amount of production we brought with us,' he told *Uber Rock*. 'We had rehearsal the day before the first show in Birmingham and we had all sorts of problems and malfunctions going on.' And there was a major spanner in the works. With just days to spare, Moose had fallen ill and a replacement was going to have to be drafted in. But with almost no time for rehearsals, they were going to need someone exceptional and the job fell to Jason Bowld. Perhaps best known to the general public for his work with Nottingham industrial-noise outfit Pitchshifter, he was known within industry circles as a superb session drummer. He had previously filled in at late notice for Fightstar – who share the same management as Bullet for My Valentine – and he was tasked with learning the entire set for an arena headline show in a matter of days. However, the band have not dwelled on the issue in the press, instead preferring to celebrate the significance of the occasion.

Anticipation for the shows was only heightened when it was announced that Bring Me the Horizon would be the main support on the tour. They were, without a doubt, the most talked about British metal band after Bullet and, after the release of their third record, *There is a Hell, Believe Me I've Seen It. There is a Heaven, Let's Keep It a Secret* in October that year, they were earning some serious critical credibility to match the attention too. Bullet for My Valentine and Bring Me the Horizon represented the two biggest acts in British heavy music. They'd even shared the covers of magazines before, most notably on an issue of *Rock Sound* where Matt was depicted holding the severed head of BMTH singer Oli Sykes – a shoot that earned Matt the ire of one Australian fan who turned up at two concerts to harangue him about the cover. But to have both bands playing on the same bill on the nation's biggest stages was a big deal.

Bullet for My Valentine had played in support of the biggest metal bands the world has ever seen many times over and they hadn't done so without learning a trick or two. Trick number one is to get the audience on your side. So at each date, the show started with a giant Union Jack obscuring the stage, as if to say, 'metal has come home.' (Naturally, at the Cardiff show, a Welsh flag was used instead.) Crucially, Bullet now had the back catalogue to justify a headline set of this scale, from the chugging opener of 'Your Betrayal' to the more measured 'Bittersweet Memories' and 'Say Goodnight' and the bulldozing, pit-inciting chaos of 'Begging for Mercy' – a brave choice of closer but one that sent the crowds in a whirling frenzy of activity. But it was the most anthemic moments, surely written in the hope that this occasion might come to pass, that lit the touchpaper of the crowd's excitement – the chorus of 'Tears Don't Fall', the harmonised lead in the middle eight of 'The Last Fight' and the symphonic structures of 'Alone'. The set even allowed for both Padge and Matt to take an unaccompanied guitar solo. Most bands are blessed to contain one great guitar player but these shows proved that, with Bullet, you get two.

The band would later remember the Manchester MEN date as the most flawless show that they had ever played; one of the rare occasions where everything goes exactly as it should. They left the stage feeling as if they'd just pulled off the impossible: '[It was our] first arena tour [...] the crowd was sold out and mental, and out of all the shows we've ever done that one was the most perfect,' Matt said to *Moshcam*. There was a slight fly in the ointment of the Wembley show when Bring Me the Horizon's set was cut short, apparently owing to concerns about crowd safety after 'Diamond's Aren't Forever' incited a massive wall of death in the middle of the standing area. But it was the show at the Cardiff International Arena that Matt would later call the most emotional moment he had ever had on stage. It was the same venue where, as a boy, he had seen Iron Maiden, Slipknot and Metallica, where he had experienced the electrifying energy and catharsis of a huge metal show for the first time and where he had seen how a great frontman could hold thousands of people rapt. His whole family were in attendance, including his eight-month-old son Evann, seeing him play at the biggest venue that his home country had to offer. 'I was saying to the crowd it's mad being on that side of the stage,' he said to the *Kerrang!* Podcast. 'Last night, it looked small. I was surprised how small the place looked. Which is maybe an indication of the sort of the big places we've been playing.'

However, the Cardiff show marked the end of a chapter

for the band and, for Matt, it was bittersweet. A dream that they had been chasing since they were teenagers had finally been achieved and there was bound to be a sense of a come-down after finally getting there. Fortunately, he had his first Christmas as a young father to soften the landing. 'I've been looking forward to that more than this even,' he said to *Kerrang!* 'Perhaps I shouldn't have said that, but it means everything to me to be a dad now, and I can't wait to get tonight over with and be a dad, be a boyfriend, be a normal person for five minutes.'

CHAPTER EIGHTEEN

AXE VOUND

After taking a break in January 2011, by February the band were back on the road again in Australia, touring the Soundwave Festival alongside Iron Maiden and Slayer. After the triumphant arena shows, they felt invincible. 'It's easy for us, we're just doing forty-five minutes and that seems like a walk in the park,' Moose said to Soundwave TV. 'Wake up, play, get drunk with Slayer.' Rob Zombie was also on the bill but, unsurprisingly, there were no reports of the band partying with him.

From Australia the band flew straight to Japan, where they were due to be supporting Iron Maiden on two consecutive dates in Tokyo. However, things took a devastating turn. On 11 March the Great East Japan Earthquake hit – the most powerful earthquake ever to strike Japan and the fourth most powerful ever recorded. The band were in the air when the tremors began and were diverted to Taiwan for the night but their crew was already set up at a hotel in Tokyo. Some of them ran; others simply accepted what was happening to them and waved goodbye to people they could see in the opposite hotel. When the band finally got to Japan the next day, the country was still experiencing severe aftershocks and they drove through a scene of utter devastation, with barely navigable roads winding through crumbling buildings. They arrived at the hotel to find that all of their crew were safe and sound but the experience left a deep impression on all involved. The earthquake and resulting tsunami ultimately claimed the lives of 15,891 people.

Unfortunately, that wasn't the only gig that Bullet were scheduled to play that year that was marred by tragedy. At Belgium's Pukkelpop in August, a storm hit the festival on the opening day. A tent collapsed, screens fell and trees were uprooted, resulting in the deaths of five people. Festival organisers took the decision to cancel the event soon after. Fortunately, there were more positive touring experiences during the summer of that year, including a month-long stint supporting Avenged Sevenfold across the US and a second-headline slot on the Sunday of Download. At the end of August, all the way until October, the band were touring the US on the Rockstar Energy Drink Uproar Festival, alongside Avenged Sevenfold, Seether, Sevendust and Black Tide. Jay was clearly enthused to be back on tour with Black Tide, who had accompanied Bullet on the road many times – one night at a Black Tide after-party, he was challenged to do the caterpillar, and ended up cutting his eyebrow open.

In November the band headed for a short tour in Mexico and South America and, while in Sao Paolo, Padge got the opportunity to show off his love for Metallica to a particularly appreciative crowd. A Brazilian Metallica covers band called Damage Inc. were playing in the Manifesto Bar in the city and, since Padge had covered 'Creeping Death' with Bullet in 2006, he accompanied the band on stage for a rendition of the *Ride the Lightning* classic.

Between touring commitments, Matt found time to head to LA and begin work with Don Gilmore on the follow-up to *Fever*. Gilmore had been an important catalyst for change in the band, so it's easy to understand why they chose to work with him again. 'Don really changed things around for us,' Padge said to *Ultimate Guitar* in 2011. 'He took a lot of pressure off us as musicians and as a band, which really helped things breathe a lot more, both musically and obviously in the vocal sessions, which is where Matt and Don really shined.' But the next Bullet record wasn't the only musical project that Matt had on his mind. In October 2011 he first spoke of a 'metal as fuck' side project and, despite remaining tight-lipped about who was involved, he was clear that it would provide a no-holds-barred alternative to Bullet's melodic take on heavy metal. 'It's far more like Slipknot or Pantera,' he told Nikki Blakk's Metal Zone. 'It's nice to step outside of that comfort zone and do something fucking ridiculous and not worry about what people are going to think, because it doesn't exist yet.' His intention was to go into the studio and create something like Slipknot's Iowa – 'just fucking violent, let it all out, no holds barred.' He did, however, assure fans in the same interview that he wouldn't be neglecting Bullet for My Valentine to pursue the project and that it would be squeezed in between the writing/recording and release schedule for the new Bullet album.

The seeds for the project were sown in July 2011, when Matt met up with drummer Jason Bowld, who had covered for Moose at the 2010 arena shows. As the pair shared a common interest in the heavier side of things, Matt had invited Bowld for a jam to see if they could come up with any material for a brutal new project; while Matt had a passion for the more extreme end of the spectrum, he wanted to get it out of his system in a fresh new setting, rather than forcing it into Bullet. But this was not to be a typical lengthy recording process of rehearsal, pre-production and then a month or so in the studio. The plan was to book a short, sharp stint of studio time and write as they recorded, producing a song a day on the spur of the moment. Spontaneity and instinct would rule the session.

And so Tuck and Bowld booked eleven days in Cardiff around December 2011 and got to work. Martyn 'Ginge' Ford was recruited to engineer the sessions and the only guiding principle was that Matt wanted to do something different to Bullet and explore different ways of working. As he put it to *Blabbermouth*, 'It was time to let my hair down and let Satan compel me.' But part of moving away from the Bullet process meant that Matt was not going to be the band's main singer. The session was focused on recording instrumental tracks and then another vocalist was going to be recruited to help steer the final sound in a new direction because, as Matt identified, with him as frontman he might as well be working on the new Bullet album and he wanted to keep the two projects as distinct as possible. And so, over eleven days, Matt and Jason wrote and recorded one track a day. It was an eye-opening experience for Matt, who was used to a far more protracted process with his main band (*Scream Aim Fire* had taken around six months). 'Writing on the spur of the moment and striking while the iron is hot captures something amazing,' he told *Kerrang!*

Right from the start, Matt had the vocalist he wanted in mind. Bullet had first crossed paths with Cancer Bats in 2008 when the Bats had supported them on an American tour run. Ever since the release of their excellent sophomore record *Hail Destroyer*, Cancer Bat's renown had been spreading globally and a huge part of their success was undoubtedly the manic charisma and guttural bellow of frontman Liam Cormier. On record, his highly distinctive and versatile voice distinguished his band from the hardcore pack and on stage he was a prowling, tireless blur of tattoos and hair. He was, in other words, the perfect choice. 'There was no one else I even had in mind,' Matt said to *Blabbermouth*. 'Liam's voice alone is just so vicious.'

Cormier travelled over to Wales to lay down vocals on the record and Jason and Matt were both impressed with the way his punk approach helped shape the identity of the band.

'When he started singing we were all like, "wow, this sounds like the guy from Rage Against The Machine," because he's got that tone to his voice,' Bowld commented to website *Festivals For All*. 'You have these shouty, ranty vocals on the top that aren't really screamo because to me screamo is one flat noise, whereas Liam's got an awful lot of feel in his voice.' Cormier spent just five days in the studio tracking his vocals.

Once the album was complete, there were only two things left on the agenda. The first was to recruit the rest of the band. The chosen bassist was Joe Copcutt, who was at the time the bassist of Rise to Remain, a metalcore act with a strong pop sensibility who Bowld and Tuck knew from the touring circuit. The line-up was completed by Mike Kingswood, guitarist in York-based quartet Glamour of the Kill, who had been recommended to the band by Ginge. The second thing on the agenda was a name, and on 30 April it was unveiled: AxeWound. Bowld credits Matt's partner Charlotte with the name but the dual meaning was lost on most people outside of the UK. As he explained to *Festivals For All*, 'I've spoken to a lot of American friends, Australian friends. You tell them "oh, the band's called Axewound" sheepishly and you sort of wait for a reaction, and most of the time it's been [an] innocent "oh great, that sounds brutal," not "you filthy bunch."' And why not? There's certainly room for more pussies in the ultra-macho world of heavy metal.

The first song revealed to the public was entitled 'Post Apocalyptic Party', debuted by Daniel P. Carter on his Radio One show. Ultra-precise in execution, yet manic and unpredictable, the song swings on a groove that hits like a wrecking ball, driven by Cormier's leave-everything-in-the-booth performance. The idea for the concept and lyrics had come from a conversation Matt and Liam had in the studio about the song's outro, which slows to a grinding crawl (Matt and Jason had actually experimented with slowing the passage down even further but decided it had gone too far and reeled it back in). The two remarked how it sounded like the end of the world, like a nuclear reactor shutting down or an atom bomb going off. That night, after retiring to Matt's house, Liam wrote the lyrics based on the idea and the next day he headed straight into the booth and laid down the vocals. The track was the ultimate statement of intent. It was clear that AxeWound were going to pull no punches.

AxeWound made their live debut supporting Killswitch Engage in Holland and, by their fifth show, they were at Download, playing the third-tier stage just under headliner the Devin Townsend Project. The band had not had much time to rehearse, owing to Cancer Bats and Bullet commitments, but Matt was typically unfazed, telling the *Kerrang!* Podcast that the band was already a 'slick, powerful machine.' And he was right. With Bowld behind the kit and two very capable musicians backing up Tuck, the sound of AxeWound in a live setting was every bit as tight and fierce as their recorded output had promised. They even snuck a storming cover of the Pantera classic 'Fucking Hostile' into the set. But the star of the show was, undoubtedly, Cormier. He tirelessly stalks the stage, keeping his head low like a boxer, clasping the mic as if someone might take it from him at any moment. Even Matt's new guitar from sponsors BC Rich, emblazoned with 'I DON'T GIVE A FUCK' along the fretboard, could not steal focus.

Cancer Bats were also appearing at Download that year but, due to the high winds (and with caution heightened by the Pukkelpop incident), the main arena opened late, meaning the band missed their slot. However, fans got a two-for-one that year. Billy Talent gave up five minutes of their main stage set to let Cancer Bats come on and play 'Hail Destroyer' and the Bats' set was shifted to a headline slot on a smaller stage anyway. The only issue was that Liam would have to play the AxeWound set and the Cancer Bats set more or less back-to-back. But Matt, who knew the worst possible outcome of overstressing your voice, had come to be very impressed with the resilience of Cormier's vocal cords.

The AxeWound album saw its UK release on 1 October 2010. The recording opens with 'Vultures', a song the whole band knew would be the opening track when they heard it, and it's easy to hear why. The riff is absolutely huge – a detuned behemoth glimmering with pinch harmonics and underpinned by Bowld's furious double-kick. It was one of the first songs that Matt and Jason started writing and ended up setting the tone for many of the album's heavier moments. In line with the unremitting anger of the music, Cormier runs on pure vitriol, the chorus a chant of 'Death to traitors / Off with their heads!' It was also the first track that Jason heard Liam lay a vocal for. As he said in an interview with

MySpace, his first thought was that it sounded like 'Rage Against the Machine on acid'. The track also comes complete with a guest solo from Avenged Sevenfold's own Synyster Gates – a wailing, discordant, mile-a-minute lead that drips with Gates's signature approach. Matt's original intention was to have a guest appearance for every track containing a solo on the album and Gates was the first player he thought of to feature. As it happens, there are no other guest soloists on the record but Tuck wouldn't have been too disappointed. As he said to MySpace, his immediate response upon hearing what Gates had laid down on 'Vultures' was, 'It's one of the best guitar solos I've ever heard.' (Mike Kingswood handled the solo live and did a damn good job of it.)

After 'Post Apocalyptic Party', track two on *Vultures*, comes 'Victim of the System'. In line with Matt's determination to try some new ways of working, he suggested to Bowld that the pair try to write a song using drums as the basis and encouraged Jason to get in the live room and lay down a couple of minutes crammed with all of his signature beats and fills. Using that as the basis, Matt then wrote riffs around the beats and the result is a wonderfully deranged slab of metal. Unsurprisingly, the star of the show is, undoubtedly, Jason with his work behind the kit, which seems to constantly vary in approach and yet is pulled off with military precision. Musically, the track reminded Liam of mid-1990s hardcore – the likes of California's Strife and Minneapolis's Harvest – and, using those acts as a cue, he decided to take a more political approach with his writing. The lyrics comment on the epidemic of homelessness in Cormier's native Toronto, where people who are clearly in need of medical attention are left to struggle and, in many cases, die on the street: 'You can hear the scream from the darkness / Just counting the days 'til she dies,' he howls and you can practically hear the injustice in his voice.

The next track, 'Cold', was the first that Jason and Matt put together for AxeWound. On the original demo Matt sings throughout the song, as opposed to just in the chorus, as he does in the final version. In many ways, this is the most Bullet-like track on offer here, with its thick, groove-based riffs and soaring hook. It was also the easiest for Liam, as Matt already had all the lyrics prepared, so he just had to come in to the session and do his thing. The track is a great showcase for the contrasting vocal styles of the two singers and also one of the most accessible moments on the album, which is, no doubt, why it was released as a single in the run-up to the album coming out. The accompanying video is a straight performance affair, with the band tearing through the track in a waterside wasteland. When you've got a band made up of hand-picked performers, you don't need much in the way of narrative to hold a viewer's attention.

'Burn Alive' is *Vultures'* fastest, most frantic moment, with Bowld channelling Slayer's legendary drummer Dave Lombardo. The track definitely has the twisted, sinister tone typical of the Californian legends, particularly in the tremolo-picked chorus part, which manages to be both wonderfully satanic in sound and also with a great hook, and the brief but blistering solo from Matt has a chaotic feel to it, much in the style of Hanneman and King. Once Liam heard the track, there was only one way to go with the words – to write about hatred, murder and doing people wrong. Sometimes the most obvious approach is the right one.

'Exorchrist' is another relatively accessible moment on *Vultures*, once again coming with a Tuck-sung chorus and a theatrical classic-metal feel. The track is a particular favourite of Liam's for the way in which Matt encouraged him to step outside of his comfort zone and try things he would never do in Cancer Bats – like the bouncing, almost-rap of the verses, or the syncopated delivery of 'Bring on the Exorchrist!' For Matt, the song was an exercise in writing in a different key, rather than relying on the open-string approach that crops up most regularly in metal, though he still sneaks in a crushingly heavy breakdown. 'Exorchrist' was the second single from the album and was released with a promo that went in hard on the occult imagery; think writhing bodies covered in blood, a bit of girl-on-girl cannibalism, a worried-looking priest and a proliferation of pentagrams. It doesn't make a lot of sense but it is undeniably macabre fun.

'Collide' is the album's curve ball, beginning with a funereal piano part that gives way to a palm-muted riff accompanied by grand stabs of synthesised strings. Tuck had clearly been boning up on his Norwegian black metal. The song came along about three quarters of the way into producing the album and was put together as a relief from all the blindingly heavy tracks Bowld and Tuck had already produced. Thematically, the song also has an interesting concept. Matt and Liam exchange verses, with Matt taking the part of a haunted victim and Liam playing a (particularly shouty) poltergeist who is pursuing him. As far as song ideas go, it's exceedingly metal but it's only partly successful. While Cormier's sections have a pleasantly nasty feel to them, as a whole the song has an air of musical theatre about it. It could almost be taken from a heavy-metal re-imagining of *The Phantom of the Opera*.

The main riff of 'Destroy' has the velocity of a runaway train and, with Bowld showing off his double-kick chops in the verses and Cormier accompanied by shouted gang vocals in the chorus, the song feels like a thrilling hybrid of metal and good old-fashioned rock 'n' roll. It's got an upbeat lyrical message too. Sure, Liam had been talking of slitting throats a few tracks prior but 'Destroy' is about letting go of your inhibitions and defeating your fears – an approach that's typical of his work with Cancer Bats.

On *Vultures*, Matt is largely happy to sit back and let Liam handle the screaming, howling, bellowing and grunting, while he chips in for the occasional melodic section. But he wasn't about to allow Liam to have all the fun. On 'Blood Money and Lies', Tuck and Cormier seem locked in a game of one-upmanship as to who can lay down the most ballsy vocals. It's Cormier who takes the prize with his performance in the chorus – he shows off a raw, gravelly vocal that's tough and melodic at the same time (he again credits Matt with encouraging him to try something different). 'Blood Money and Lies' was one of the first demos that was put together for the project and it's a real album highlight, especially with the fiery anti-establishment spirit of the lyrics. With that said, while Liam begins exhorting you not to 'pledge allegiance to your own moral death,' he does end up at 'fuck me, fuck you, fuck everything,' so perhaps he's just pissed off.

The album closes with another offbeat moment that could have so easily turned into parody. 'Church of Nothing' rides on a galloping power-metal riff reminiscent of Helloween, which Bowld described to MySpace as a 'metal jig' – but fortunately, with a delirious thrash verse and Cormier's trademark bark, 'Church of Nothing' manages to be ferocious without trading in any of its fun.

Vultures might have been put together in a fraction of the time Matt was used to when it came to making albums but nothing about it seems thin or rushed. If anything, it's a bewildering outpouring of ideas that feels for all the world like Matt letting off a serious amount of steam and, with Bowld's technical excellence and Cormier's ultra-distinctive voice, it makes for a hugely entertaining listen. It's by no means flawless – the album tends to falter when it moves into more melodic territory and, lyrically, some of it is a bit metal-by-numbers – but at no point does it feel like an undercooked side project. It's a fully realised body of work with its own identity and character, at times catchy and at times crushingly heavy.

Much of the press were impressed too. *Vultures* got a four K write-up in *Kerrang!* and *Metal Hammer* gave it eight out of ten. The BBC said that 'Vultures isn't an album we'll be talking about twenty years from now, but for thrills, spills and hair-raising heaviness, it gets the job done in style.' (In reality, the album's status as a 'side-project' is probably the biggest threat to its legacy, rather than any issues with quality.) *AllMusic* probably summed it up best, saying, 'Packed with harmonized guitar riffs, chugging breakdowns, and pinch harmonics galore, the band nails its colours to the mast with an album that feels like a loving tribute to all the things that make groove and thrash metal so fun.' Not everyone loved it: *PopMatters* felt it failed to distinguish itself from Bullet's output, writing, 'It defies all logic to begin a separate project and for the most part pepper it with sounds and ideas that are already synonymous with your name.'

Ultimately, the AxeWound star burned bright but brief. After a brief skip around the UK, the band were scheduled for a headline tour of the US but it had to be postponed due to visa issues. It was never rescheduled, no doubt owing to commitments with the members' other bands, and AxeWound have not played again since. Matt has expressed a desire to return to the project and it stands as more than just a footnote in the Bullet story. It would have a heavy influence on the way in which Bullet for My Valentine would go about making their next album but, where AxeWound was a short, sharp and exciting diversion, Bullet's next step would prove to be altogether more difficult.

CHAPTER NINETEEN

MUSICAL THERAPY

Shortly after recording had finished on the AxeWound record, thoughts turned to the follow-up to *Fever* and Matt had been deeply influenced by his experience in the studio with Jason and Liam. He no longer felt that a long pre-production process was necessary in making a great record; it was simply time and expense that Bullet were now experienced enough to bypass, as he explained to Andrew Huang. 'We'd gotten to a point in the career that I felt we didn't need to waste time doing that anymore,' he said. 'The traditional way is you write songs over a bunch of time, you do demos, then you do pre-production with a producer, then you re-record all that stuff; and it just seemed like such a long-winded, boring, expensive process, when this is our fourth full-length record – my fifth including the

AxeWound record.' It was also felt that it would be good to get away from the distractions and commitments of the UK. Since an associate of the band's management had recently purchased a full recording facility in Thailand, Matt, Moose, and Martyn 'Ginge' Ford flew out for a combined writing and recording session.

Karma Sound Studios is in Bang Saray, a small fishing village on the northern tip of the Gulf of Thailand, about two hours south of Bangkok. The studio is something of an oasis, complete with its own gardens, swimming pool and even its own kitchen staff to prepare meals. There's little within the walls to distract you beyond the tropical climate – and should you want distracting, a white sandy beach is just minutes from the door. For Tuck and Moose, the appeal was obvious. They could fully immerse themselves in the process of writing for the album and have the studio on hand to jump in whenever inspiration struck. Being family men, it was only natural that they wanted to spend time in Wales with their children but the distractions of home could get in the way of making an album.

Matt was hoping to imitate the process for *Vultures* and that meant dedicating himself to the studio. The approach started to bear fruit almost immediately. On the morning after they landed – which was, coincidentally, Valentine's Day – and with jet lag kicking in, they went straight to the studio and tracked the skeleton parts to what would, ultimately, become 'Breaking Point'. Plus, once all had settled into the process, they flew their families out to be with them anyway. As Matt said in an interview on Nikki Sixx's Sixx Sense radio show, 'We had our cake and ate it.'

Don Gilmore arrived at the studio shortly after Tuck, Moose and Ginge. He had not been available for the first four or five days of the session due to commitments with another band but, when he arrived, it felt like a reunion of old friends. As Matt told Scuzz TV, it was all 'high fives, hugging, and bro-downs.' However fractious those first few weeks were on the *Fever* sessions, all of the tension had dissipated and Gilmore was now a full inductee into the Bullet gang. 'Having that bond and trust and friendship – it made everything so much easier, and quicker,' adds Matt.

The intention for the album was to continue in the same melodic vein as *Fever* but this time to slow the songs down, rather than relying on speed as a means of creating force or momentum in the song. At first, slowing songs down proved difficult for the band, as they were so accustomed to tearing through tunes at breakneck speed (they were, after all, raised in the school of thrash metal). 'It felt a bit uncomfortable to play, which is odd,' Matt told *ARTIST Direct*. 'You'd think the faster things are, the more uncomfortable they'd be. It was actually the reverse.' The aim was not to make the album more accessible but to make it sound 'bigger, heavier and fatter.' Carrying through the methodology of stripping things back that had proved so successful on *Fever*, bludgeoning riffs were going to be used with restraint and dropped in only where they needed to be. Moose was also looking to complement the songwriting with a more classic approach to his drumming, having listened to a lot of Led Zeppelin in the lead-up to sessions. Out were huge crazy fills at every opportunity; in was a natural sound, free of the triggers that had given his drums their machine-like quality on previous records.

A big cue for the new album's direction had been taken from *Metallica*, otherwise known as *The Black Album*. It is a record Tuck has been very much open in his admiration of in the past. 'You wouldn't necessarily call it a heavy album, but the sound of it is fucking heavy, big, and it sounds timeless,' Matt commented to the Voice of Rock Radio. 'We're trying to take that theory of slowing down, putting less technical bits in and concentrating on the vocals and the meat and bones of the song.' Accessibility might not have been the end game but *The Black Album* did become Metallica's best-selling album, clocking up a mind-boggling 30 million physical sales worldwide. You wouldn't have blamed Tuck if he had that fact in mind when seeking to take inspiration from it.

Not that the band were all business while in Bang Saray; they did take some time out to sample nearby Pattaya's notorious nightlife. '[We] saw all the bullshit you'd wanna see… there was ladyboys and ping pong shows and all the crazy stuff,' Matt told Poland's *Rockville*. 'It was a bit grim and seedy and a bit smelly and stuff, but as far as an experience goes, it was fun.' Moose had an eye-opening experience when he saw a woman insert a pen in her vagina and write 'Welcome to Pattaya'. 'Her pussywriting was neater than my handwriting,' he said to *Metal Injection*.

With the drums and the rhythm guitars laid down in Thailand, the pair returned to the UK and reunited with Jay and Padge. (On returning, Moose actually re-recorded many of the drum tracks from the Thai sessions, feeling that he could've played with more confidence.) Padge had spent some time with Gus G – Ozzy Osbourne's current guitar player – and Andy James from Sacred Mother Tongue, a progressive-metal act hailing from Northampton. Both have reputations as gifted shredders and, in jamming with them and playing some of their material, Padge felt that his horizons had been expanded and he was open to some new ways of trying things. But while Bullet's earlier work (and particularly *Scream Aim Fire*) had been marked by Padge's exceptional lead-work, solos were not going to be a big part of the new album. Matt felt that it was easy for metal bands to get carried away with arrangements and begin to think of them as the most important part of the song, when, as he commented to *Noisefull*, 'they are not'.

Vocals were also finished in Wales, in part at The Atrium, where some work had been done on *Vultures*, and in part at Rockfield Studios in Monmouthshire. The experience was considerably different to that of *Fever*, where Don Gilmore and Matt would together tear down and rewrite parts up to five times in searching for the perfect version of a given song. This time, Gilmore let Matt sit back and handle it himself and, for Matt, it was a signal as to how far he had come as a songwriter – he had no doubts that Gilmore would step in if he felt he needed to. Lyrically,

Matt was drawing inspiration from much more personal places. Where typically his approach would be to use a real-life situation as a starting point and then take it off into the realms of fantasy, this time he was looking within the dynamics of the band for content.

As would later be revealed, friendships were starting to fray as the band neared the end of the touring cycle for *Fever*. At the time, the band stopped short of going into specifics but the quartet had begun to drift apart and were no longer spending time together as friends. 'There was a lot of stuff going on behind the scenes with me and the guys that was … it wasn't ugly, but we started to drift apart for the first time in nearly fifteen years,' Matt told *Rockville*. 'It's more just capturing the frustrations of those moments rather than anything else. It was almost like a little therapy session, without having to have therapy... It was a frustrating record to make.' Moose revealed that it had got to the point that the band needed to sit in a room and vent their frustrations with one another, to clear the air and move forward as a unit.

By the time the sessions came to a close, the album had been written over four different locations, with many songs written and discarded along the way; of particular importance to Matt was that the album hung together as a whole, rather than containing individually strong tracks that did not sound alike. Around the time that AxeWound were preparing to release *Vultures*, playing festival slots and making videos, the fourth Bullet album was being mixed, once again by Chris Lord-Alge and, just as the AxeWound saga was winding down, with Matt riding high off some great reviews and strong live shows with a new band, the Bullet for My Valentine machine would roar back to life.

CHAPTER TWENTY

TEMPER, TEMPER

Bullet for My Valentine appeared at Radio One's Rock Week in October 2012 for a world premiere of their first new material since 2010. The song was called 'Temper, Temper' and, as the tremolo-picked riff kicked off the fourth-album cycle of the band's career, they certainly sounded like they were ready to build on the success of *Fever*.

'Temper, Temper' was the last song tracked for the album and one of three that appeared on the final release that had not been written in Thailand (the drums had been written in Bang Saray but the guitars and vocals that first accompanied it were scrapped and rewritten). The original intention was not for the song to be the lead single of the album – in fact, it was meant to be a free giveaway track, released as a download on the band's website. But right from the start, it was clear that the song was a step in a new direction for Bullet. The working title for the song had been 'drum and bass' and it's a good illustration of where changes had been made. Gone were the blast beats, double-kicks and furious pace of old Bullet – this was a mid-tempo rock track hung off a syncopated verse groove, with an upbeat singalong chorus destined for rock clubs. It was, for want of a better phrase, a party track, built around two simple parts and devoid of the complex interlocking riffs and harmonised leads that had become the band's trademark. And, despite the title, it didn't really feel angry. Lyrically, it was celebratory, about releasing negative energy in a positive way.

Response to the track was curious. It took off on radio, getting onto the playlist of many mainstream stations and, no doubt, reaching way more ears through that channel than Bullet had ever found before. But, on the other hand, some of the core fanbase were none too pleased about the change of approach and they took to the band's YouTube channel and Facebook page to let it be known. A typical exchange went something like this: one fan comments, 'Not impressed, going from fever album to this? Smh [shaking my head]'; another retaliated, 'Fuck all of you. This song is awesome.' A music video followed shortly after – the first to not feature the band in performance. The clip was set in an anger-management class – a rather unsuccessful one, as the attendees end up going wild and wrecking the room. It is, in many ways, the perfect video for the song – fun, a little silly and rather forgettable.

If some factions of the fan base were unhappy with how far Bullet had strayed from the formula, the next single to be released from the album wasn't going to do anything to appease them. 'Riot' was another track recorded late in Wales and had come about from a riff that Padge was messing about with in rehearsal. It wasn't even close to a metal riff; it had more of punk or pop-punk about it. But it had caught Matt's ear exactly because it didn't sound like typical Bullet for My Valentine fare and the band set about constructing a track around it. Because of its strange offbeat repetitions, the band took to calling it 'Lead Frog' or 'Lead Elephant', in reference to its leaping or stomping quality; Padge described it to *Thrash Hits* as 'backwards moshing'. It had been a real change of attitude for the band to work with something so simple – the main riff is essentially one note – but Matt felt that the simplicity of the music brought out a strong melody in the vocal. For many of those who heard the album prior to release, 'Riot' was, apparently, a standout track.

At just over two-and-a-half minutes, it's a brief blast of energy with elastic guitar work, a huge hook in the chorus and a cheeky nod to Judas Priest in the lyrics. Simple though it is, no one individual part outstays its welcome. A video was filmed in New York, showing the band walking through the streets and gathering a crowd behind them like heavy-metal Pied Pipers, who eventually convene to see the band performing under a swinging bulb. But Bullet were not a new band and there was no escaping the fact that the new material was going to be compared to the old. Once again, there was a significant amount of noise online about Bullet abandoning their roots. Even the fact that Matt had cut his hair short was taken as a sign that the band had turned their back on metal.

But Bullet for My Valentine were sticking to their guns. A band has to evolve and try new things, and it's not as if they were strangers to drawing heat online. 'These days, especially on the Internet, people don't tend to go for changes very much and it seems the fans kind of wanted us to stay the same, which is kind of weird,' Padge said to *Thrash Hits*. 'As musicians, the last thing we want to do is churn out the same songs and the same sort of music, so people have to understand that we like to keep it fresh and change it up for ourselves as well.'

Temper, Temper was released worldwide on 8 February 2013 and, whatever reservations some Internet critics might have had about the new sound, Bullet had by no means abandoned their roots entirely. Take opening track 'Breaking Point'. There are riffs flying left, right and centre, with Moose propelling the track on a busy beat accented by a cymbal bell. From the angsty yet melodic chorus to the heavy breakdown and the delirious solo, it's got everything that had made Bullet popular in the first place. 'Breaking Point' is the track that most directly refers to the elevated tensions in the Bullet camp at the end of 2011 and was a favourite of Matt and Moose's for the very fact that it had all the key Bulletisms present and correct. Indeed, you could make the argument that 'Breaking Point' would have been the safer single. It's still catchy and radio friendly but has enough anger and tension to keep the core fan base happy.

'Truth Hurts' is the third song that wasn't written in Thailand and it's also one of the most exposing songs Tuck has ever written. It openly discusses a downward spiral of drug use and, this time, it's not from a third-party perspective, as it was on 'The Last Fight'. '[It's] delving into the darker side of being in Bullet, the rough times,' Matt commented to *Scene Magazine*. 'Drinking too much, experimenting with drugs, being a bit too rock 'n' roll. It's letting people know that it is an amazing lifestyle, but at times it can be a dark, lonely place, especially if you're not enjoying yourself. It's a shitty place to be when things get tough.' It's a brave account to put on a record, openly stating you need 'one more line to make me feel like I have something left to give,' and the song is, ultimately, about facing the reality of the situation – the first step in overcoming it. With Moose's militaristic drumming and a winding hammer-on riff, the intro is Bullet through and through. The big melodic breakdown and exchange of singing and aggressive vocals in the pre-chorus would sit quite happily on *Fever* and 'Truth Hurts' feels all the stronger for it.

After 'Temper, Temper', the album takes a left turn into more mid-tempo territory with 'P.O.W', a brooding number shooting for anthem status. With a stuttering groove that carries through the chorus and a quiet-loud dynamic, it nods to the alternative rock of the 1990s and the emotive, pleading chorus immediately imbeds itself in your subconscious. The song is based around Matt's experiences of anxiety attacks and sleep paralysis, whereby the sufferer awakes mentally but is unable to move or speak – a condition that often comes in conjunction with hallucinations. However, Tuck is wise enough to keep the lyrics ambiguous and the theme of self-imposed imprisonment, as raised on 'Truth Hurts', are carried over here. Much like 'Temper, Temper', it's also structurally very simple, being built around a few chord progressions and melodies with little of the extravagant guitar work listeners had come to expect, though the strength of the chorus ensures it has everything it needs to remain powerful.

Not that Bullet were entirely ready to retire the guitar wizardry, which makes a pleasing comeback on the chugging intro to 'Dirty Little Secret'. By the time a disembodied yell ushers in the grooving riff, it sounds like the band are putting their foot down and heading for top speed but the track veers off a cliff and into a melancholic verse. The pre-chorus is wonderfully tense, with Moose rolling around the toms as if the song is crumbling at the edges, and the chorus takes things up a notch again. But, ultimately, 'Dirty Little Secrets' can't seem to decide what it wants to do. By the time the second chorus has come back around, the song switches back into ballad mode before moving into a minor section underpinned by a twinkling piano line. You can't criticise the band for experimenting with new textures and structures but 'Dirty Little Secret' feels like a somewhat unsuccessful attempt to blend the band's metal heritage with its wide-ranging ambitions.

'Leech' kicks off with a ballistic snare roll that Moose had, in fact, picked up from The Rev (James Sullivan) while touring with Avenged Sevenfold, but the similarities end there. The track's a pretty generic rock affair that does nothing to particularly offend, nor anything to distinguish itself. There's very little by way of interesting guitar work, save for in the breakdown, and the segues from verse to pre-chorus and chorus feel laboured. Where much of the album has been marked by lyrical soul-searching up to this point, Matt's anger is directed externally on 'Leech' – the song is a diatribe about the sycophants and hangers-on who surround the band – but he fails to muster even half the bile he has on older songs that address similar topics. 'Your invitation, it doesn't exist / So tell me why you keep crashing the party,' goes the chorus; it sounds more like a playground exchange than something from the raging, murderous imagination that fans had come to know and love. Just one album ago Tuck was bleeding his victims from the heels. Now he was asking people to leave his party. It's easy to understand why the album felt a little toothless for some.

But not all of *Temper, Temper* veers wildly from the formula. 'Dead to the World' is a song of two halves: the first part is a classic rock ballad sprinkled with emotive leads but, come the midway point, the song rides a tough palm-muted riff into a fret-bothering discordant solo before closing on an arena-ready singalong. It's not 'Nothing Else Matters' and it isn't quite 'Bittersweet Memories' or 'Say Goodnight' either but it is a neatly constructed song filled with plenty of ear-catching hooks and great guitar work and, therefore, a more than fair addition to Bullet's relatively short list of slower material.

Lyrically, the song was a collaboration with Chris Jericho – WWE superstar and lead singer of the rock band Fozzy, who had supported Bullet in Canada in 2010. The pair had stayed in touch ever since and, when Matt experienced a touch of writer's block with the track, he reached out to Jericho for help. 'It was one of the last songs we wrote,' Matt explained to *ARTIST Direct*. 'It reminded me of an old-school metal style, very much like a Metallica track from *Ride the Lightning*. It's very heavy and melodic, but ballad-y at the end. I thought, "Who do I know that grew up in that era and loves that kind of music?" Chris was an obvious choice so I called him up.' A day later, Tuck had a message on his answering machine, containing lyrics and a melody for the verses and choruses (the song's huge closing moments – probably the highlight of the song – were penned by Tuck himself). Tellingly, Padge told *Thrash Hits* it was the closest track on the album to classic Bullet – and also one of his favourites.

The band's experiments with more of a hard rock-type sound vary in effectiveness throughout the album but, with plenty of angst and some double-kick drumming from Moose, 'Saints & Sinners' has a bit of an edge over some of the material on the album. It's another party track that shows the band aren't afraid to have fun and they smartly set it at the perfect tempo for jumping up and down in a sweaty club. In the 'Lock! Load! Fire Away!' refrain, you're reminded of how adept a hook writer Tuck really is and the vibe of the track suggests the band had looked to the swaggering attitude of their pals in Avenged Sevenfold. The influence of Synyster Gates can even be heard in Padge's solo.

Bullet for My Valentine have never been shy in expressing their admiration for Metallica, so it's really not such a surprise that they opted to do as the Godfathers had done with 'The Unforgiven II' and produce a sequel to a track. The only question was, which one? While in Thailand, the band posed the question to fans on their Facebook page and the answer was overwhelmingly in favour of one song. The result was 'Tears Don't Fall (Part 2)'. Just as Metallica borrowed both thematically and musically in producing 'The Unforgiven II', Bullet here employ the same quiet-loud dynamic through the verses and the chorus as heard on 'Tears Don't Fall'. The guitar tone of the opening lick is almost identical and it's hard not to raise a smile to Tuck's cry of 'Let's go again!' that ushers in the rest of the band. You could perhaps criticise 'Part 2' for not distinguishing itself enough from the original. Structurally, it's almost identical and the lyrics don't develop any particular narrative arc from part one. But, in creating a song that clearly recalls the first while also being completely distinct, it's an impressive feat.

The final song of the album is also its best and, much like 'Truth Hurts', it's a track that cuts right to the heart of the tension that was floating around the Bullet camp at the time and the indulgences that were getting the better of the band. 'Livin' Life (On the Edge of a Knife)' actually came about on one of the less productive days in Thailand, where frustration was setting in, so Matt and Moose stepped away from the session and had a couple of drinks. Tuck came back to the guitar somewhat tipsy and busted out the intro riff for the song – a syncopated lick with an eastern flavour to it. While the riffs and chord progressions are very simple, Matt's vocal carries the song entirely, stretching into the upper reaches of his range for the discordant pre-chorus before launching into the finest chorus on all of *Temper, Temper*. It's proof that the simplest songs can produce the strongest melodies, as Matt himself had asserted.

Temper, Temper was released on 8 February 2013, debuting at number thirteen in the Billboard 200, eleven in the UK charts and four in Australia. But, following the uncertainty that had circulated on the Internet with the two singles, no one could say for sure how the album would be received. In many ways, Bullet were due a critical mauling. In taking their brand of commercially-savvy metal global, they'd attracted the ire of many a dilettante but the resounding success of all their album releases up to this point had meant that they were more or less immune to the slings and arrows of the press. However, for many reviewers, *Temper, Temper* was a misstep.

Some were positive – notably, *Kerrang!* gave the album four Ks, calling it their most mature effort to date. *Loudwire* also praised the band for positively channelling the friction they had experienced, saying, 'Rather than letting things fester, they turned lemons into lemonade by allowing it fuel the creative process.' Others were lukewarm – the *NME* called it 'clinical and precise rather than mind-blowing'; *Drowned in Sound* argued that 'levelling criticisms of unoriginality or lack of innovation and evolution at bands like BMFV is almost redundant. They're judged on the size of their hooks and in that department *Temper, Temper* largely delivers.' But *The Guardian* perhaps best summed up the way that the album would come to be regarded in a two-star review that criticised the album for its 'ever more sanitised version of their trademark sound,' saying, 'The dark heart that powers the best heavy music is conspicuous by its absence, despite frontman Matt Tuck's frequent attempts to portray himself as an angry young man.'

In truth, with another band's name on the cover, *Temper, Temper* would be a good album. A band are fully entitled to push and pull their sound in whatever direction they wish and, between *Scream Aim Fire* and the AxeWound record, Bullet and Matt had traversed the more extreme territory many times over; so, they were left with the only option of moving more towards the middle ground. There's no denying that the band know how to write a brilliant hook, a soaring chorus and a searing lick so, in stripping back their sound, there was no reason to think that they shouldn't try to channel their abilities towards a big rock record. But the fact is that Bullet for My Valentine work best when they are combining the sweet and the sinister, the angry and the affirmative, the brutal and the pretty – it is, after all, the essence of their name. Despite its title, *Temper, Temper* doesn't have nearly enough anger or darkness to offset the more pop elements of Bullet's approach. It's ironic that, at a time when the band was experiencing its most turbulent period, the album they produced came out sounding tame.

CHAPTER TWENTY-ONE

RAISING HELL

ullet hadn't toured as a unit since 2011 but, never ones to slack off when it came to road duties, they wasted no time in getting out in support of *Temper, Temper*. They kicked off with a show in Cardiff with The Smoking Hearts in support (featuring none other than Jay's bass tech, Calvin Roffey). They followed up with stints in Australia and Europe. In Birmingham they played the O2 Academy, where the show was filmed for both the 'P.O.W.' and 'Breaking Point' videos, which would be released in May and June, respectively. Following that, they headed to America to headline the HardDrive Live Tour.

In both Europe and America they were supported by Halestorm – a Pennsylvanian four-piece fronted by Lzzy Hale, who had been attracting a lot of attention for her powerful stage presence and voice. Fans on the tour got a special treat in Bullet's set during the rendition of 'Dirty Little Secret', when Lzzy joined them on stage to take over vocals from the second verse. The collaboration was a shrewd move by both Bullet and Hale, as the addition of Lzzy adds another dimension to this tale of lust and adultery. 'It's definitely one of the highlights of the set,' Matt commented on Eric Blair's *Blairing Out* show. 'It's not something we've done a lot. We did a couple takes of it in the soundcheck before the first show and we've done it every night since.' Matt was clearly impressed with Hale's skills too: 'She's amazing, she's very inspiring, a beautiful person inside and out, she's very talented... the perfect woman.' At this stage of touring, *Temper, Temper* was getting a fair airing in the setlist. Of the fourteen-song set they played at HardDrive Live, around four were taken from the latest release.

Summer brought with it festival season and, judging by the band's schedule, it's not a season they'll soon forget. Bullet played, among others, Rock am Ring, Rock im Park, Greenfield, Nova Rock, Hellfest, City Sound Festival, Graspop Metal Meeting, both legs of Summer Sonic in Japan, Lowlands and, of course, Download (their only UK festival date that summer). For Moose, however, this sixth Download appearance was the best. Since they were flying in and out again, many of the band's family came to support them so it had the feel of a hometown show. Even though they were certified veterans of the event, Jay still had a 'pinch me' moment when he stepped on stage. 'I remember being in the crowd before Bullet and thinking, I wanna be up there. It's a dream come true,' he told HUNOW TV. The band played under Slipknot on the main stage and, from walking on to the strains of 'O Fortuna' to the flames that erupted from the amp stacks during set closer 'Tears Don't Fall', they looked every inch the heavy metal band finally come of age.

The band headed off to the States again in the latter half of the year, though there was a special break in September when Matt married his long-time girlfriend and Evann's mother, Charlotte. But, where there had been a long three years between *Fever* and *Temper, Temper*, by autumn that year the band were already talking to the press again about the prospect of heading back into the studio. This time they would be spending a few days with Terry Date, the legendary producer behind a host of famous contemporary metal acts, most notably Pantera and Deftones. It was only a tryout to see if there was potential for a collaboration and no more was ever said of the meeting, so we may never know what Bullet for My Valentine with a dash of Deftones would sound like.

But it wasn't just talk of heading back to the studio. The band had put their money where their mouths were and had been laying down new material. At the end of November, ostensibly to help promote the UK arena tour that the band were going to close the year with, they announced a new one-off track entitled 'Raising Hell'. It had been recorded at Metropolis in London and the band would later reveal that they felt the need to respond to some of the criticism they had been facing for *Temper, Temper*. And what a way to do it 'Raising

Hell' was. Opening with dissonant, drawn-out chords while Padge leans on his whammy bar, the track soon gives way to the most crushing groove that Bullet had rode since 'Waking the Demon', with Matt's vocal doubled and harmonised in a way that recalls the glory years of 1970s metal.

What's remarkable about 'Raising Hell' isn't that it pulls anything particularly unusual out of the bag. It has a half-time, melodic chorus, an intense screaming passage in the second verse and a screaming solo: the elements Bullet had used time and time again. It's that it delivers everything you'd associate with a BFMV song in the purest, most perfect form, as if they'd somehow cooked down all of their best songs into one four-minute slab of unadulterated pleasure. It's hard to say where 'Raising Hell' came from – perhaps heading into the studio without the presence of a producer freed them from the pressure of trying to adapt their sound and, in returning to what they knew best, they hit on a new vein of inspiration. Either way, you can't deny the joy of a huge thrash riff paired with a Matt Tuck chorus and a Padge solo. It's simple maths and, if fans had been turned off by *Temper, Temper*, 'Raising Hell' was a very promising sign of things to come. Even the accompanying music video seemed to suggest that the band were going back to basics. The four members are depicted in black-and-white, just as they had been in the video for '4 Words (To Choke Upon)', playing in the round with nothing else to distract from the performance.

For the second time, Bullet fans were to get the early Christmas present of a December arena tour, with the band heading to Manchester, Glasgow, Birmingham, Wembley Arena and Cardiff. With the announcement that they had officially become the biggest British metal band since Iron Maiden, the headline run was packaged as the Rule Britannia UK tour and came with support from two young UK bands: Asking Alexandria and Young Guns (the latter, in particular, had been making waves stateside with their second album *Bones*, which was recorded at Bang Saray's Karma Sound Studios). Moose, in particular, was looking forward to taking back what was his, having missed the last arena shows.

Once again, Bullet used 'O Fortuna' to mark their entrance, with the crowd illuminated by a disco ball that shot pinged light around the arena, before the band tore into 'Raising Hell' accompanied by enough pyrotechnics to raise the dead. A particular highlight of the set came in the form of a five-song medley, taking a defining song from each album: 'Hand of Blood' segued seamlessly into 'Room 409', before a marked shift of tone into the longing of 'Hearts Burst Into Flame' (sadly stripped of the intro); 'Begging for Mercy' also made a brief appearance in Padge's solo, before the chorus of 'Riot' closed out the career-spanning mash-up. It's interesting that 'Riot', a recent single initially marked as a huge potential breakout, only got a thirty-second airing. It was one of just three songs from *Temper, Temper* in the set, along with 'Dirty Little Secret' and 'Temper, Temper', indicating that less than a year from the album's release, its material was already falling out of favour with the band.

During the encore, the band even took the time to pay

tribute to their forefathers with a cover of 'Ace of Spades' by Motörhead. At Wembley, the song got this particularly potty-mouthed intro from Matt: 'We're not usually a band that plays a lot of fucking cover songs 'cos we like to play our own shit but, to celebrate British fucking music, we thought, "Let's play a fucking song by a British band that pretty much wrote the rulebook on rock 'n' roll, ripped it up, took a shit on it, then fucking burned it."' Whatever you want to say about Bullet, you can't deny that they know how to pick their covers. On paper, it's hard to imagine Matt doing a good job of imitating Lemmy's signature gruff drawl, so he doesn't even try, and his voice sits on top of the frantic, speeding riffs perfectly. The band would march off the stage to the sound of 'We Are the Champions' by Queen and those in attendance were certainly in agreement.

But, while the performances were impeccable, there had been something of a dip in Bullet's wide-reaching appeal since their 2010 arena tour. Reviewers in Manchester, Glasgow and London all commented on the somewhat low attendance for the tour in otherwise positive accounts of the show. One writer for *The Guardian* said that 'keeping British metal in arenas seems to be more a case of making a statement for Bullet for My Valentine than a necessity.' And, as time went on, it became clear that there was more uncertainty from within the band about the release of *Temper, Temper* than it had initially appeared. In a telling interview with Dutch online magazine *FaceCulture*, released in January 2014, Padge and Moose seemed clearly unhappy with some elements of the *Temper, Temper* process. Both agreed that they felt the album was somewhat rushed and that some of the songs could have been made better were there more time. Padge remarked that he felt the demos were 'dry' and 'a bit basic', saying that, in the past, they preferred to fill space – though he also added that he liked the mix and thought Matt's vocals were 'great'.

Padge was also concerned that the wrong songs had been released first and that, had a more traditional Bullet track been the lead single – preferably 'Breaking Point', with its guitar-driven approach – more people may have been primed to give the album a chance. But perhaps the most obvious bugbear was the Thai recording session that Moose and Matt attended alone. 'I feel if four of us were in a room together, it would have been a much stronger album,' Moose said. 'Rather than mainly two people doing it. I think if we were all in the room getting the vibe... the songs would have been the same but a lot better, and a lot catchier.' Moose also insisted that the next record would be produced in the same manner as the first three.

Bullet had never been short of critics but they had always had success and momentum on their side, steadily growing in popularity and maturity from their first EP to *Fever*. But *Temper, Temper* represented the first time that they had to confront the possibility that their latest release had not been a step forward, either commercially or artistically. It was a blow for the band but they were by no means down and out. In a separate interview with German TV programme *EMP Rockinvasion*, released in February 2014, Matt seemed to acknowledge the criticisms surrounding the album, while defending the decision to take things in a new direction. 'I wouldn't change that record for anything – that was the record we wanted to make and that's what we should be doing,' he said. 'A rule that we've always stuck by since day one is we do it our way, or we don't do it at all. Someone else fucking your career is not acceptable, but if you fuck up your own career, at least you can sleep at night.'

Bullet were no longer untouchable. Previously the undisputed champions of contemporary British metal, they were going to have to fight to retain the title. But they had battled their way out of a decade of utter obscurity; they had defied every critic and naysayer and won over a legion of fans across the world, one show at a time. The next chapter in their career was going to bring big changes but it was also going to prove that Bullet for My Valentine had plenty of fight left in them.

CHAPTER TWENTY-TWO

REBIRTH

On 27 September 2006 Bullet for My Valentine stopped off at Lake Buena Vista in Florida for a show at the House of Blues. They were hotly tipped and gaining momentum; a band being caught up in the midst of something bigger than them. It was their first major headline US tour following the runaway success of *The Poison* and they were out on the road with Bullets and Octane and Escape the Fate. And they had no way of knowing that an important part of their future was standing in the audience, even though he wouldn't come into the picture until almost a decade later.

Sixteen-year-old Jamie Mathias was in Florida on holiday with his parents but he was actually a Welsh lad himself, having grown up in Abertysswg, about forty miles north-east of Bridgend. *The Poison* had been doing the rounds at his school, with Bullet for My Valentine not just one of the most talked about bands in Britain but boys from the valleys too. So when he saw they were playing in Florida, he grabbed himself a ticket and went along. Sure enough, he was blown away by the technical display, especially as he himself was an aspiring musician.

He had started playing guitar at the age of eleven and, like most young men with an ordinary life and too much time on their hands, he quickly buddied up with his childhood friend Chris Green to form a band. His father had introduced him to the likes of Black Sabbath and Metallica and, eventually, shown the pair the essentials of playing the guitar (Mathias's first riff was 'All Right Now' by Free). Soon enough, they had recruited other members into the fold and were cutting their teeth on the local pub scene with covers of Thin Lizzy, Ozzy Osbourne and T-Rex.

Slowly but surely, the band began to develop their own material and build up a following for themselves, eventually adopting the name Revoker in 2006 (they'd spent years arguing over names, eventually settling on Revoker for its connection to cards and because 'we'd had enough,' as they said to *Hit the Floor Magazine*). In grand tradition, the band spent the next few years learning their craft, touring hard and writing as much as possible.

While recording sessions for an EP in Newport, they ran into a familiar face from the scene – Benji Webbe from Skindred, keen to see what all the beautiful racket was about. After sharing his admiration for the band's classic sound and thick-set riffs, he came on board with the band in the role of producer, introducing them to the kingmakers of the South Wales rock scene, Martyn 'Ginge' Ford and Geoff Rose. Webbe worked closely with the band to help hone their sound, ensuring that every riff was finely tuned and every hook delivered with conviction to make the songs as strong as they could possibly be. He even employed some slightly unorthodox approaches to ensure that the importance of songcraft was hammered home, sitting the band down and forcing them to analyse 'The Winner Takes It All' by Abba. And so, in between working day-jobs, the band completed work on a debut album.

Revoker's first choice of labels to send the album to was legendary imprint Roadrunner Records and, unbelievably, they were also the first to get back to Revoker and indicate that they were interested. It had caught the ear of a certain Monte Conner, the Senior Vice President of A&R, who had been responsible for signing the likes of Machine Head, Slipknot and Trivium, though he had never signed a band from the UK before. Impressed with what he had heard at a show in Manchester (and with Roadrunner having narrowly missed out on signing Bullet and possibly still smarting), he snapped the band up. For all the world, it looked like the Revoker's dreams were coming true.

Benji Webbe again handled producer duties on Revoker's debut album for Roadrunner, entitled *Revenge for the Ruthless* and released in May 2011. A strong collection blending hard rock and heavy metal, the sound had a common thread with

Bullet, probably from the shared admiration for Pantera, Slipknot and Machine Head. With plenty of mid-tempo headbangers built around fat and unfussy riffs and tied together with clinical drumming, it was an admirable debut effort. But the star of the disc is, undoubtedly, Mathias. His highly dextrous vocals could switch from an Anselmo-like growl to a mid-range snarl in an instant and he is also gifted with a clear and crisp upper register that, at times, recalls his mentor Webbe's, even bordering on the screeching power of Skid Row's Sebastian Bach.

Just like Bullet, they weren't afraid to get on the road and do the work required to build a fan base the old-fashioned way. Support slots followed with the likes of Rob Zombie (with whom there were no reported fallouts), Chimaira, Sepultura, the Cavalera Conspiracy and Drowning Pool – a run in which they also shared the stage with Fozzy, the vehicle of Matt Tuck's good pal Chris Jericho. During an appearance at Sonisphere, the tent had to be shut due to overcrowding and, turning up at Graspop Metal Meeting for an 11.30 a.m. slot, they found two thousand riotous Belgians screaming their lyrics back at them. *Revenge for the Ruthless* had not even been released in Europe yet. The year peaked with a date playing alongside Mathias's childhood hero Ozzy Osbourne, where they were the only support. Heading into 2012, the band had strong new material ready to record and tours with Anthrax and Fear Factory to continue spreading the message.

However, for every tale of local lads turned into global superstars, there are thousands of tales of bands who almost made it, and so it turned out to be for Revoker. In 2010, Warner Music Group acquired all of Roadrunner Records, a process that began when they purchased majority shares in 2006. By 2012 Warner was making substantial cutbacks across the operations and roster of Roadrunner, including the permanent closure of the UK offices. Many of Revoker's closest links to the label were laid off and it left the band 'in limbo', as Mathias put it to website *WalesOnline*. Revoker's second album would never see the light of day and, come 2014, Mathias was working at a car dealership in Newport, another victim of music-industry machinations beyond his control. But one evening, while working a night shift, he got an unexpected text message.

It was March 2015 and, one month prior, Bullet for My Valentine had announced the shock departure of Jay James. A courteous but guarded statement had been released, declaring, 'Jay has been a part of this band for well over twelve years and part of our lives forever, and we're gonna miss him as much as we know you guys are too. We wanna wish him all the best and success with whatever he chooses to do next and will always be grateful for his contribution and sacrifices he made for this band.' No further information had been offered as to the circumstances surrounding his departure; 2014 had been an exceptionally quiet year for the band, who had fulfilled some sporadic tour dates in the first six months and then largely laid low. Fan forums and comment sections were awash with speculation and tributes to James but the Bullet camp was remaining tight-lipped on what the future would look like, apart from assuring fans that a new album was in the works and that a replacement would be announced when appropriate.

Unbeknown to the public, Jay had not been a part of the band since July. Mathias had known Padge for a number of years and the text he received was an invitation to audition for the vacant position in Bullet for My Valentine. It was a no-brainer: Revoker was on permanent hiatus and, while Mathias had been a guitar player in his former band, he was a more than capable bass player too. So he put a tape together to send to Bullet and was promptly invited to head down to London and audition with the band in person.

Mathias was relatively relaxed during the process. He told a film crew that was there to capture the moment that 'he was excited more than anything... at the end of the day, it's just jamming with a few boys. That's what it's all about.' His relaxed attitude was clearly working in his favour. 'His audition tape was flawless, so we thought, "OK, this guy's really good!"' Tuck would later say to *Revolver*. 'But then he came in and just completely smashed it. He wasn't fazed by anything – we were actually filming it for a documentary, so there were camera people there – and he was just awesome.'

For Matt, the synergy was immediate. Not only had Mathias been in a signed band before and, as such, had experience of playing live, recording, press and the rigours of touring but he was also a born-and-bred Welshman who had been raised in an identical climate to the rest of the band. Everything right down to his accent was in line with the rest of the crew.

And, crucially, he had a great vocal talent that could really lend itself to Bullet's live show. As Tuck would later tell *Metal Hammer*, 'he plays like a beast and he sings like an angel.' After the show in Florida back in 2006, Mathias had waited outside the venue to meet the band. He'd shaken Matt's hand and told him he would know the name of his band in a few years' time. Some nine years after that first meeting, Tuck and the rest of Bullet formally invited Mathias to join them.

To date, the band have not been forthcoming about exactly what happened with Jay, preferring to keep the details private. In an interview with *Revolver*, Tuck did say that 'parting ways with Jay was the most difficult thing we've ever had to do,' making it clear that Jay was not just a bandmate, he was a best friend. Three months were spent deliberating over the decision and 'fighting and fighting to find valid reasons for him to stay.' While avoiding going into detail, he did comment that 'it was in Jay's best interest personally, more than ours, that he was not in the band. People can read into that what they want, which they will anyway; but it was just stuff going on that was jeopardizing the band's career, and it had to stop.' Jay had been an integral part of Bullet for My Valentine from its very inception. Matt said it best himself to TherapyTelevision: 'He's one of the boys, we all grew up together, we all experienced everything together from going to school to puberty, chicks, growing up, music, rock 'n' roll, being in a band... it goes way back.' For better or for worse, Bullet would never be the same again.

CHAPTER TWENTY-THREE

ARMED TO
THE TEETH

Writing for the new album had actually begun way before Jay's departure. As early as October 2013 Matt had been speaking of new songs that had been written for the follow-up to *Temper, Temper*, with four or five having been put together while the band were on the road. And where paring songs back to their most essential elements had been the approach that they had favoured on their last efforts, this time they were going for all-out attack. 'We're very much concentrating on musical ability, we're showing off basically!' Matt told *Ultimate Guitar*.

One thing that was clearly going to change for the recording of the fifth record would be the means by which it was made. In a candid interview with *Metal Hammer*, the band spoke of their experience of recording *Temper, Temper* in Thailand and Matt's decision to begin that process with Moose alone. Padge, in particular, had been hurt by the decision. 'It really pissed me off, to be honest,' he said. 'Being told over email that you're not going to Thailand to record an album with your band... I'm sure it'd piss anyone off. I was fucking confused, hurt, and just didn't understand it.' Moose also took the opportunity to express his discomfort with the situation, stating that, while his relationship with Matt was healthy, he 'felt bad' about leaving Jay and Padge behind. For his part, though, Matt maintained that the decision was the right one; Matt has long been acknowledged as the key decision maker in the band and here he defended his right to make a decision that wouldn't necessarily be popular, saying, 'It's always in the interest of and for the good of the band, not just me as an individual, and there were certain things going on that people needed to sort out.'

Nonetheless, almost every element of the recording process was going to be different this time. No doubt bolstered by the lively response to 'Raising Hell', which had been self-produced in London, the band opted to return to what they knew best. The new album would be recorded in the UK and songs would be put together over a long period of time, with a traditional pre-production and demoing process, rather than written in the studio. For most of 2014, Matt, Padge and Moose were holed up in Padge's private home studio in Bridgend, slowly bringing songs to fruition, working meticulously, yet organically, to write the songs together. Indeed, the writing process was the most collaborative that the band had ever undertaken, with Padge and Moose writing a lot more than they had ever done before. The fact that they were back in their hometown was also having a positive impact. It was the first time since *The Poison* that they'd undertook the main bulk of writing in the UK and, where in the past they'd felt the need to get away from their everyday lives in order to focus on recording, this time the result was a more harmonious environment. 'It was just very relaxed,' Matt told *Guitar World*. 'Everyone was in a good mood. There wasn't that feeling of being locked in a studio a million miles from home and being pissed off because you don't want to be there.'

Padge had come to the sessions 'armed to the teeth' with riffs and lead parts, not wanting to ever be found short of something to offer when it was required and Matt was sticking to his role as a rhythm player more than ever. 'For the last two records, Padge has really stepped into that role of being the lead guitar player,' Tuck said to *Guitar World*. '[...] It was good not to have to worry about that other stuff. Padge is such an amazing lead player in his own right.' The album would be the first ever to contain no lead playing from Matt, who also took care of bass playing duties for the record.

The result of this complete change of approach was that the band entered the formal recording process with more songs already written than they had ever had before. Clearly, they were not taking their position as established UK rock giants for granted. They had a sense that they needed to prove themselves again and they were more than willing to graft to do it. The only missing piece of the puzzle was who to get on board to handle production duties.

During the writing process for the album, Matt, Padge and Moose had been listening back to the EP, *The Poison* and *Scream Aim Fire* and they heard what had gone unnoticed for a long time – the special energy and magic that those records embody; the sense of a band doing what came most naturally to them, rather than reaching for something else. The band had flown out to the States to meet with other producers but, upon returning to the UK, also met with Colin Richardson and discovered that the bond that had been forged over the recording of those albums was still very much intact. Since the band were aiming to capture the raw fury of their earlier releases, it made sense that Colin should be behind the desk to do it.

However, they were not merely looking to recapture old glories. The band has long been outspoken in its belief that they should and would adapt and evolve as they grew older and a part of that meant working with new people. As such, in an official Facebook post, it was announced that the record would be co-produced by Carl Brown. Brown had worked on a whole host of projects alongside Richardson, including Trivium's *In Waves* (co-produced by Martyn 'Ginge' Ford), Rise to Remain's *City of Vultures*, Machine Head's *Bloodstone & Diamonds* and Carcass's *Surgical Steel*. What's more, almost an entire album's worth of material had been demoed but dropped for not passing muster in the eyes of the band. Some of the demos had been more in the classic-thrash mould, similar to *Master of Puppets* but, not wanting to re-tread territory that they had covered on *Scream Aim Fire*, they had been scrapped in favour of a more modern approach. 'We wrote a couple of songs and came up with an edgier, more modern style of metal,' Moose told *Metal Hammer*. 'And it was just like, "This feels fucking great, let's roll with it."'

Since the band were using signposts from their past to head to new, harder places, the onus was on Matt to go there lyrically too. Some of the more lyrically extreme material that had been a huge part of the band's approach in the past had been toned down in more recent efforts and Tuck felt it had was time to revisit that frame of mind. The only issue was he was no longer an angry young man fighting for his seat at the high table of rock. He was happily married, a father and a success. 'I think the last couple of albums… the team has been let down slightly in having real content which has an emotional connection with myself, you know?' he said in an interview with *Loudwire*. '[…] I think a big part in making that come to reality was having lyrical content, which was emotionally challenging for me. So, revisiting places that weren't so good when I was growing up. Like my early teens and coming through young adulthood, stuff like that. Just being picked on and not taken seriously.'

Getting into the right frame of mind to revisit those emotions he felt as a young man – of being an outsider, of having to fight to protect his right to be himself – was no easy task. After all, being himself had helped him sell millions of records. But, once he got into the flow, he found that it became easier and that the material was appropriately dark to accompany the ferocity of the music. 'I was having a hard time at school, getting my ass kicked by guys for being a super-skinny, pale dude with long hair into heavy metal,' he told *Metal Hammer*. 'I became an easy target. It was about feeling those emotions and trying to recapture that frustration and fear and anxiety and work that into a song.' The key thing was that, this time around, the lyrics were to focus on real-life experiences and emotions that listeners could relate to. 'I know that there are some kids who can definitely relate to it, and I know there are men and women like me who have had it before, or still have it at work, or whatever,' he added. 'The whole point of this album was to try and make it as real as I possibly could, to try and connect with someone out there.'

With a renewed passion for the classic Bullet approach to making albums and a conscious effort to muster the aggression and passion that they felt had been lost over the last album, the reports from the studio were that Bullet were at work on their heaviest, most intense record yet. 'Working with certain people and producers in the music industry, if you've had a radio hit at one time in your career, they try and make your whole album sound like that,' Moose revealed in an interview with the *Hartford Courant*. 'We tried to do that on the last album, and we failed miserably [...] You think, "Maybe if we tone it down a little, we'll get even more success." But I don't think that's the case in heavy music at all.' The band sensed that their fan base was clamouring for them to find some piss and vinegar in their sound again and this time they were promising to deliver it. In fact, Matt was hinting that it was easily the angriest and strongest record the band had ever made. It would be called *Venom*: a clear message that the Bullet who put together the assault of *The Poison* had returned to take what was rightfully theirs. It was music to the ears of fans.

CHAPTER TWENTY-FOUR

INJECTING SOME VENOM

The first taste of Bullet's new material arrived on 18 May 2015 – the same day that Mathias was announced as Jay's replacement – and it's hard to imagine how Bullet for My Valentine could have made more of a statement. From the opening scream of 'No way out!' it's clear that the track of the same name has no burning desire to garner radio support or to expand Bullet's fan base with a more accessible approach; its only aim is to be a blisteringly heavy, devastatingly effective slab of riff driven, contemporary metal and it achieves it within the first minute. The riff is short, tight and performed high up the neck, so it sounds fraught and panicked. Moose is slamming on the kick drums like he's trying to stamp out a fire in his soles. Matt alternates between a furious roar and a threatening growl, before taking off into melodic territory for the chorus, which is shot through with the tension of the main riff. And Padge shows why Matt left all lead duties to him after the breakdown, delivering a restrained but scorchingly fast solo that's perfectly in keeping with the anxious tone of the song. Lyrically, Matt clearly had taken himself to darker places – 'Oh my God is this really the end? / I guess I'm not all right / I just can't tell what is real anymore / I'm trapped in my own hell,' he sings in the second verse, simultaneously summoning themes of madness, hallucination and death.

The response was immediate: the YouTube lyric video lit up with comments about the return to form, notching up almost a million views in short order. With the vicious modern edge that had been added to the classic-metal influences the band had so ably adapted in the past, there was a sense that Bullet might be about to deliver something huge and it didn't go unnoticed by the band. 'It was a relief to be in the good graces of heavy metal,' Moose told the *Hartford Courant*. 'It was a huge weight off our shoulders.'

On 30 May 2015 Bullet for My Valentine made their return to the live circuit, headlining London's Camden Rocks Festival at the Electric Ballroom. Over 200 bands were booked to play in venues all over Camden but Bullet's return to the stage was, without a doubt, the biggest news of the festival. It was the first time the band had played live in over a year and their first time ever with Mathias handling bass duties. With a capacity of just over 1,000, it would be a more intimate environment than the band had been involved in for a long time. As well as providing a suitable warm-up show for the new boy, it also allowed the musicians a chance to debut some new material to a hardcore block of fans.

The band opened with 'No Way Out', showing that the track was every bit as crushing live as it was on record, but it was deeper into the classic-heavy set that the performers really showcased their new asset. Mathias has a lead singer's chops and the versatility to handle all the vocal-support duties that the back catalogue requires. Not only is he possessed of a hair-raising scream, he also has the range to take care of the harmonies too. The result was a more powerful sounding band, one that now has the ability to do proper justice to its melodic elements in addition to the heavy sections, which it has always delivered with relish.

The occasion of the Camden Rocks headline set also allowed the band to debut another new song, 'Broken'. Opening with a riff that sounds like mortar fire before moving into a lightning-fast, palm-muted riff that flares around the fretboard, it continues in the same vein as laid out by 'No Way Out'. It's ferocious and hard edged in a thoroughly contemporary way, while offering all of the elements that defined Bullet during *The Poison* and *Scream Aim Fire* eras. With angsty and melodic verses and a grooving chorus interspersed with moments of discordant savagery, it couldn't be further from the large-scale rock of *Temper, Temper*, especially by the time the double-time thrash breakdown kicks in, accompanied by a furious solo. For many in attendance, it was yet another sign that Bullet were ready to reassert themselves on the scene. As *Team Rock* put it, 'The ecstatic response that greets the likes of "Tears Don't

Fall", "Scream Aim Fire" and "Waking The Demon" underlines the considerable impact that they've had on our world – while promising, heavy newie "Broken" hints that they may well have steered themselves back on course.'

Camden Rocks turned out to be the only show that Bullet would play in London for the rest of the year, with the band heading off to South America before supporting Slipknot, accompanied by Lamb of God, at the Summer's Last Stand tour across the US. Slipknot were a band that had made a serious impression on Matt when he saw them in 2002 and he held them as the bar for an incredible metal show for a long period, so it was high time that Bullet were booked on a tour in support of the Midwest's most terrifying band. The UK tour announced for that year would take place in many of the towns and cities across Britain that the boys had typically been missing out in recent years – proof that the band were ready, willing and able to prove themselves once again.

On the US tour, the band were also tasked with carrying two very special tokens. Two young fans, James Simmons and Corran 'Coz' Powell, had died in a car accident in December 2014; Corran's brother had contacted the band asking them to take the men's ashes out on the road with them and they agreed. Two pieces of jewellery were made to hold the ashes, with Padge taking the lead in looking after the remains. 'It's never been asked of us before, but it's such a beautiful gesture,' Tuck commented to *Billboard*. 'It makes you feel a bit funny inside.'

The next single from *Venom* was released on 24 June,

accompanied by a video directed by Stuart Birchall. Opening with a chanted chorus that sounds from the very start like it's destined to become a set staple, the song explodes into a hypnotic descending riff. Thematically, it's a clear message about resisting abusers and the most earnest expression of Matt's resistance of schoolyard tormentors to date. Despite easing off the anger from 'Broken' and 'No Way Out' – it's slower in tempo, more morose with an atmospheric middle-eight section – it is still possessed of a righteous indignation. If more proof were needed that the band had a newfound desire to explore darker themes again, the video is a hard-hitting tale of domestic violence and revenge; one that pulls no punches in its depiction of cruelty. While the song was drawn from Matt's experience at school, it's good to see the band opening up the song to wider interpretations. 'We were all keen on making a bold, dark statement about abuse that would resonate with a wide audience,' said director Birchall.

By the time the album's next single rolled around, entitled 'Army of Noise', there was no doubt that the band were back to full speed, producing some of the best music they'd ever put their name to; refined, mature and demonstrating a real songwriting craft but with all the force and power of their earliest material. Rattling along on a thunderously fast and low riff, 'Army of Noise' fits roughly into the category of Bullet's 'party' tracks but is blessed with a chorus as good as anything the band have ever done – all palm-muted chromatic runs and trilling vocal hooks. While Padge has never been a slouch when it comes to putting thrilling solos on tape, 'Army of Noise' shows him at the peak of his powers, delivering a lightning-paced, eastern-flavoured lead that sounds something like Dimebag Darell jamming in a medina. This might be Bullet letting their hair down but there's nothing soft or middle-of-the-road about it; it's fast, furious, and undeniably fun. It's no wonder Matt chose to pay tribute to the fans with the lyrics.

All signs were pointing to one undeniable fact: that Bullet for My Valentine were back. Emerging from the longest writing-and-recording process that they had ever undertaken to complete an album, they had emerged with *Venom* and it was every bit as deadly as its name would suggest. *Kerrang!* gave it four Ks, noting that, out of the troubled genesis of the album has come renewed focus and determination: 'Rather than sounding like a depleted force marshalling themselves for final showdown,' writes Nick Ruskell, 'what you get here is a champ raising himself to full height again after a moment of taking his eye off the ball, and reminding you what a devastating force he is.' *Metal Hammer* were equally impressed and noted the cathartic undertones on an album preoccupied with persecution: 'This is a grown up, more mature record from four men who are now in their thirties looking back at the pain of their former selves,' writes Luke Morton. 'With every guitar stab, every snare hit and every scream, the past pours out of Bullet into their music in pure metallic fury. It's music therapy for band and fan alike.' The review pegged *Venom* as the band's best album since *The Poison*.

Bullet's road to *Venom* had been a long one. It had taken

them almost ten years under a different name to even get signed. They had graduated from local shows in pubs and community centres in their native Bridgend to arenas in Japan, South America, the USA and anywhere else you could put a pin in a map. They had survived a two-year touring cycle that almost cost Matt his voice, they had endured critical disdain and they had weathered the disappointment of fans as they evolved their style. They had not come out of it unscathed, losing a founding member along the way. But *Venom* proved that Bullet for My Valentine still had fangs.

BFMV's story is, in many ways, the archetype of 'making it' as a rock band. They began as boyhood dreamers, learning to play in their bedrooms by imitating their icons, and they worked and rehearsed and slogged until the world took notice. They may even prove to be the last heavy metal band to do so. The musical landscape is so different now that it is hard to imagine a band so brutal going so far, particularly when there is little money available in the industry to promote anything but safe, dependable, investable mainstream acts. But maybe there is hope for the rock 'n' roll fairytale yet. As Matt told *Westword* in 2008, 'If you do it long enough and you're good enough, it's only a matter of time before someone acknowledges it and it can't be ignored anymore.'